T0196283

Reinventing Leadership

Personal Guide to Recognizing Your Own Leadership

Margaret-Jane Howe

authorHOUSE®

AuthorHouse™
1663 Liberty Drive
Bloomington, IN 47403
www.authorhouse.com
Phone: 1-800-839-8640

Published by AuthorHouse   9/21/12

ISBN: 978-1-4772-2612-4 (sc)
ISBN: 978-1-4772-2622-3 (e)

Contents

PREFACE

Good leadership is the key to a successful life for every individual. Competent leadership is necessary for the financial success of every business. Excellent leadership fulfills employees while satisfying stakeholders. Successful organizational leadership influences long term health, wealth, and happiness of internal and external contacts with the organization. The quality of leadership has a wave impact on others. Leadership is a critical issue.

Leaders are truly valuable when team members are aligned to their vision, strategy, and direction.

When people ask me why I wrote this book, it's from understanding the value of good leadership, and from evidence that good leadership is not undertaken as often as it could be. My primary readership is people in business who are leaders, who want to be better leaders, or who aspire to leadership positions.

More people could develop leadership ability if they understood better the requirements of good leadership. Others may awaken to their unconscious leadership ability and improve their sense of self-worth by new recognition of how valuable they truly are.

Reinventing leadership is about techniques and approaches. It's also a highly personal book on how to become more aware and how to choose to shift old ideas. Reinventing leadership is also how to release old beliefs, gain more personal satisfaction, and career advancement.

Reinventing leadership may develop better communication abilities and thus better leadership ability.

For some leaders, this reinventing leadership book will have them think about every day actions to improve leadership outcomes by changing a few things here and there. The process of reinventing leadership is not to say there is anything wrong or inadequate about anyone and the way they do things now. Reinventing leadership is rather a way of reviewing individual behaviors. It's an opportunity for a person to know *how or what* to change, a process easy and obvious once it's recognized.

Evolution to becoming a competent leader is a personal development one day at a time; one challenge, one practice, one communication, one failure, one success at a time. The more you work at it the better you become.

Leadership is also influenced by the rest of the team, the followers of the leader. It's smart leadership practice to surround yourself with high caliber people with differing personality styles and create a balance of styles.

Leadership has become my profession. It's a lifetime interest.

Leadership opportunities in business strategy and implementation, mergers and acquisitions, financial restructuring, and business turnaround showed me the impact of good versus mediocre leadership. In many situations, such as IT systems implementation, sales, and project management, the quality and effectiveness of leadership is the difference between success and failure.

At times, despite lack of good leadership at the top, leadership germinates joyously at different levels in an organization. Team members are self-motivated and effectively influence others by building good relationships, improving communication and understanding. Team members who instead struggle to achieve such positive and effective influence can change tack to steer in the right direction by reading 'reinventing leadership'.

I am motivated to be able to help business people find their way to successful leadership through increased understanding of not previously understood perspectives they may have held about themselves and others. More behavior choices come from increased knowledge and understanding.

When I thought about it, the difference between a great experience in a business organization and a ghastly one is the key ingredient of leadership ability and awareness.

Bad leadership, lack of leadership or poor leadership skills kill off the possibility of employees enjoying their work.

By contrast, competent leadership causes a service business, for example, to function effectively when employees receive management respect which is reflected in customers receiving a great service experience. Leadership willingness to access continuous improvement knowledge and act upon it, can turnaround negative situations fast.

In many businesses, negativity comes from the top. How the business is led from the top has the most influence on whether the business is profitable and maintains a winning culture with leading market position. Leadership is the most likely ingredient for business continuity and long term success.

Even with the handicap of bad leadership at the top, you can't put super good people down, and it's possible to get pockets of goodness and satisfaction in any organization. A sustainable organization however is determined by who controls its future. It's ultimately those in charge.

The unseen impact of decisions goes far beyond the decision of one person, team, or organization. This is not legalistic interpretation of leadership responsibility. It's one of environmental and social sustainability awareness. We have only just begun to touch the surface in understanding sustainable business and to realize how critical successful leadership really is.

My view of what constitutes successful leadership is not necessarily similar to those who rewarded UK business leaders with pay rates 145 times the average employee salary rate in 2011. Nor would I concur with ten per cent of total personal income being taken home by the top 0.1 per cent of earners in the USA.

Reading my book, you will see leadership for me is about taking responsibility for communicating effectively and inspiring others. Leadership is about creating opportunities for everyone to become effective in their sphere of influence. It's about being able to reward each person for being an effective leader instead of the top of the pecking order individual 'take all' approach.

Enabling others to do well is a business leadership choice which provides wealth outcomes such that everyone is able to be well remunerated, and the environment is respected, in a sustainable long term business financial model. Over the longer term, growing the business leadership skills and abilities of all employees generates higher returns to stockholders, and to all stakeholders. Caring for the environment sustains life on the planet for all.

Some ideas are provided in this book as a first step in looking at your own personal leadership and how effective it might be to have a good attitude, to practice personal awareness, and act upon your findings.

With the title of leader comes the responsibility to play fair, rather than be greedy and abusive. There is no need to be a pig in a trough. I work with many excellent business leaders and they don't need a king's ransom to turn up to work every day.

The more successful others are – the more successful you will be. How do you cause a high level of leadership success? You learn to understand how to deliver a superlative team performance – starting with working on you!

How did I get to be so vocal about this to write a book?

I noticed over the years some directors and managers changed very little in leadership styles and behaviors. The fallback position was maintained at 'doing what we've always done'.

People don't do things badly because they want to. Bad habits happen because people aren't aware of their behavior, they possibly fear change, and often don't realize there is a more successful option. It sometimes takes looking in the mirror to see what you're putting out there onto others.

I also recognize many people don't realize how great they are.

Everyone is the possibility of being a leader, we don't need to wait for someone else to ask us to step forward and take up leadership.

This led me to consider writing a leadership book for people who could benefit from learning to recognize their own worth. To write for people who wanted to become better leaders and didn't know how. And to remind directors and management who rise to high places that the responsibility doesn't lessen as we get more experienced and 'wiser'. The buck still stops with you.

If your business or your life is not working, or not working as well as it could, then it's your leadership which can change things for the better. If your life isn't working, blaming other people and external circumstances is a cop out. YOU can do something and change your life or your situation. Start now to get it on track.

We all need reminding of 'back to basics' success fundamentals.

Life can be tough, it can be rough, it can be soul destroying, boringly routine, and dull. Reinventing leadership can renew your awareness and open your eyes for the first time in an area you hadn't thought about before.

Reinventing leadership can remind you of who you are underneath the shell you might be holding out to the world to hide your talents and vulnerability.

You might be living a life out of habits that worked once and don't work today. You might be frustrated with a situation and not able to improve it. Or you might benefit from some general help to get on track again. Read this book and save yourself the cost of a business consultant. Think better of yourself. Find an activity or change of attitude to spur yourself into action and have the life you've always wanted to enjoy.

When I saw how I had been hiding myself under a bushel, I took action too. Several years ago I decided to change profession and trained in the USA to become a Master Business Executive and Leadership Development Coach, affiliated with the International Coaching Federation (ICF). I now train others to see their situations from different perspectives so they can master leadership effectively and grow profitable businesses confidently.

I conduct niche development workshops and training seminars for emerging leaders. I work with senior business leaders to modernize their leadership style by retraining and providing in-house strategic planning seminars. This new leadership development role enables me to enjoy empowering others to succeed and command their future success.

It delights me when my clients see that no recession, taxation difficulty, tight fisted bank, seemingly unproductive employee situation, or 'somebody else' is holding them back once they start to work with me. If you want to succeed in leadership – just discover who you are and take the right action.

I hope you enjoy reading Reinventing Leadership – Personal Guide To Recognizing Your Own Leadership. Meet me at one of my training seminars soon. To your enjoyment and success! Good luck.

ACKNOWLEDGEMENTS

Thank you to those who gave feedback and helped to edit this book making it an easy and helpful self-help book to refer to repeatedly.

Thanks go to Helen Thompson and Mandeep Lakhan my script editors, Omar Ayche for unstinting honesty, Carmel Greenwood for her author's review, Dawn Bates who pushed me to the publishers, and Gwen Hustwit (book cover designer). Graphics were provided by Alicia Yao and artists Huhulin, Kacpura, and Onime at Dreamstime. My gratitude also goes to my children Katie Larsen, Jessica Larsen, and Sam Larsen for their unstinting support with whatever I do.

I've been blessed by terrific leadership role models, at home, work, socially, politically, multiculturally, and economically. With much appreciation of all these contributions, I now offer you my service to leaders the world over.

1.0 LEADERSHIP CONTEXT

1.1 Introduction

Leadership occurs when behavior causes an impact on others. Impact can be caused consciously, or unconsciously.

The power of leadership comes from within. The power of leadership oozes outwards, impacting everyone around. If you're not feeling anticipation of the leadership you're stepping into with inner calmness, excitement, and self-knowledge, then either there's no awareness of your leadership or you're not in touch with who you are.

Effective leaders know who they are and where they're going. They have what it takes to lead in a given situation. Whatever each day may bring, leaders know they're in the right place at the right time. Leaders don't question their ability. They know themselves as leaders. While some tasks may be rough and tough, others cause exhilaration and inspiration, causing powerful action and change. Life as an effective leader is dynamic and momentous.

When someone mentions leadership, we often think the word relates to "someone else", such as Winston Churchill, Mahatma Gandhi, Lee Iacocca, John F. Kennedy, Nelson Mandela. You might think of more recent leadership examples such as Angela Merkel, Barack Obama, Condoleezza Rice, George Soros, Hugo Chávez, Marjorie Scardino, Mikhail Gorbachev, or Oprah Winfrey.[1] We *know* these people as the personifications of leadership.

---

1 See under "Famous Leaders" at the end of the book.

- Do you recognize YOURSELF as a leader?
- If you DO recognize yourself, are you SATISFIED with your leadership?
- On a scale of 1-10, where are you below the 10 mark of best leader?
- What kind of leader are you?

Take a minute or two to think about the questions above and make notes for yourself.

You may or may not be the kind of well-known leader who hits the media headlines. You are a leader all the same. Leadership is signaled in all kinds of ways.

Peoples' perceptions of leadership are as diverse as the colors of a kaleidoscope.

Leadership is available to anybody. Sometimes you don't even know how much of a leader you are. When leadership is understood, it's easy to see yourself as a leader, to be seen as a leader, and to access better leadership. Forget the idea that leadership is someone else's role. If you still think that, you don't yet recognize who you really are.

1.2 Expression of Leadership

Start
by discovering how to source your own inner leadership abilities

Leadership Quality and Effectiveness

Lead
by focus of energy & commitment, to bring ideas into reality

Continue
by recognizing opportunities to exercise leadership

©Alicia Yao, M-J Howe

So you want to become an extraordinary leader?

Extraordinary leadership is about:

SELF-KNOWLEDGE – RESPONSIBILITY – COMMITMENT

Ideas of leadership are often unconsciously formed by examples of inspiring leadership in other people. Do you know what aspects of leadership in others cause you to be inspired?

Take a moment or two to make a note of your thoughts. What is it about someone else that inspires you? How does their action and way of being inspire you? What is it about that person that you wish you could be?

A leader with focus and commitment, for example, attracts *some* followers. If that person also has integrity and compassion, *more* people are attracted to follow such a leader. With focus and commitment, integrity and compassion, a leader is being born. Add to that a well-rounded personality with charisma and fun, an inspiring and memorable leader is born.

HALLMARKS OF AN INSPIRING AND MEMORABLE LEADER

- FOCUS
- COMMITMENT
- INTEGRITY
- COMPASSION
- CHARISMA
- FUN

PEOPLE FOLLOW LEADERS WHO LIVE THE FUTURE THEY WANT

People are inclined to follow leaders who are being the person they want to be and who they believe can take them to the future they want.

Such inspiring leaders, by their very nature, attract followers. Visions, ideas, plans and proposals presented and communicated by such leaders naturally become reality. Leaders can also provide the opportunity for others to lead by the leader's ability to listen and validate what someone else says.

You can ascertain whether you're an inspiring and memorable leader **by evaluating the measurable results** of your leadership.

How clearly do you see your own leadership style, evaluate and understand it's strengths and weaknesses? A leadership style is discovered, as the very best leaders discover, by continually questioning assumptions. By continuous observation of the results of their actions, leaders gain more understanding of what's happening and what's possible. Constant review followed by renewed and expanded effort leads to extraordinary change and results. This is the art of leadership and how to continually inspire yourself and others.

YOUR DRIVE TO CREATE WHATEVER YOU WANT WILL REMAIN STRONG IF YOU KEEP GENERATING IMPROVED OUTCOMES BY CONTINUOUS SELF-ASSESSMENT

Outcomes are only limited by your imagination. It's up to you to decide what to dream. Why not dream of what you want and get on with getting it? If you're not there yet – keep going!

As a leader, it's important that you always **believe**. As the famous cartoonist Walt Disney once said: "If you can dream it, you can do it."

The key to success is to form dreams, goals, ambitions, and aspirations and make them happen. Anything is possible! It's even possible to discover the solution to something which might seem impossible right now! All you need to be a powerful leader is to open up mentally and be willing to see new aspects of the same things. YOU ARE capable of being a GREAT leader who is the possibility of having a powerful impact on your life and many others.

Now let's go learn about you, your leadership styles, and your aspirations for leadership.

The quality and effectiveness of your leadership is important for you to achieve your own life satisfaction. This leadership quality and effectiveness is even more important to others. Leadership is not only about you and your needs; it's about the lives of *others* whom you are privileged to lead.

See yourself reflected in the impact you have on others. Read on. I'll explain more as we go along.

Life experiences are there for the taking if you go after them. Depending on your attitude, experiences can be varied, challenging, or interesting. Be warned, leadership is a constantly changing experience.

1.3 So What Is Leadership?

Leadership describes a situation where you go in front and act inspiringly, such that others follow. Leadership doesn't exist if no-one believes your viewpoint, follows your directions, or joins in the event you want to cause. Leadership is about causing something.

Leadership is by definition leading and guiding others. It's being in front of and directing the movements of others. Leadership can involve conducting another person by hand or by your behavior, guiding them by using persuasion and influencing their actions or opinions. Leadership can cause others to go into action or it can lead others astray. Leadership is seen as a result of something. It's about having first place in a situation, for example, acting as leading counsel. Leadership is also where one is enticing others to go farther than was intended by them or you. Leadership is a preparation for action or acting to introduce something new. Leadership can be directing conversation towards a point of view or conclusion. It can be about taking a leading place. Are you starting to recognize how leadership occurs?

Some schools of thought suggest some people are leaders and some people are not leaders. Some suggest leaders are *discovered* when the going gets tough and, under pressure, people step up to lead others out of calamity.

But all that stands between someone being a leader and not being a leader is letting go of old beliefs: letting go of holding back your individual natural expression and, at the same time, allowing others the safety to be themselves around you. Letting go and authentically being yourself creates the possibility of leadership.

Any expression of any person has impact on others. Remember **anything** done or said has the potential to influence others. Whether you *inspire* others to follow, or you *make a request* to be followed, people will choose at their own discretion and pace to follow or not.

Your behavior is always the possibility of being influential. A leader is recognized and followed by recognizable and influential traits. The proof lies in who takes notice and what they do about it.

As a leader, you are responsible for your example, your style, and the content of your communications. How you do this will be a strong determinant as to whether others follow and how willingly they follow.

The ultimate choice to follow is with the potential followers; as is the responsibility for their choice.

A LEADER CAN BE WILLING TO LEAD

A LEADER CAN BE ABLE TO LEAD

A LEADER ACCEPTS THE ROLE OF LEADERSHIP

BY PROVIDING AN EXAMPLE OTHERS FIND ATTRACTIVE TO FOLLOW

We're now getting related to some concepts of *what is leadership*. By now there's a sense of familiarity with some, or all, of these ideas. Now, in order to make a difference and become a leader who makes things happen, we need to consider the context of leadership at another level:

- Learn to try out styles of leadership
- Influence the positive self-expression of others around you
- Be yourself in leadership in a way you haven't been before
- Become comfortable with leadership
- Have leadership be the most powerful communication tool you have
- Understand and practice leadership
- Have your leadership be an easy contribution to every area of your life
- Become a visionary leader, consistently bringing about what you say

1.4 Extraordinary Leadership Skills

Master ten keys to extraordinary leadership. Learn how to:

- Create and communicate from a true leadership context
- Recognize leadership paradigms
- Get new insights when assessing results
- Be a silent and astute listener
- Turn criticism into a positive learning experience
- Be reflective and thus be a source of wisdom
- Reinvent leadership consciously and continuously
- Be goal-focused
- Choose your reactions, learn how to play with choice
- Plan and know how to develop effective strategies

The answers to these key areas will become apparent as you read through the examples in the book.

Remember:

EXTRAORDINARY LEADERSHIP REQUIRES

SELF-KNOWLEDGE – RESPONSIBILITY – COMMITMENT

1.5 The Leadership Context

Leadership is demonstrated in every action of every day.

As stated previously, **inspiration** is an essential aspect of leadership which causes others to follow a leader. A leader sees a future direction and is able to cause others to *desire that future direction*. Some people are motivated by the *benefits* they believe will derive from going in this direction. Other people are inspired to follow or join the leader, who they *believe* will deliver the perceived benefits to them. The decision power is with the people.

Clearly, **credibility** plays a key part in this type of effective leadership. If people *believe* the leader is capable of generating the desired outcomes for them or with them, leadership is more likely to be effective and powerful. Credibility is not about whether someone is telling the truth in this context. It's about whether people who consider the options of whether to follow the leader **believe this leader** can deliver on what seems to be promised.

In this leadership context, credibility delivers a <u>communication</u> which aligns with the world of listeners.

Ask yourself if your communication makes sense to **others**?

When you look at it, there are many situations where someone becomes a leader such as father, mother, sister, brother, teacher, politician, manager, chairperson, flight captain, research scientist, technologist, orchestra conductor, sportsperson, astronaut, inventor, business entrepreneur, orator, writer, team leader, market developer, trader, or altruistic benefactor. Any of these roles has the propensity to cause another to follow the lead, and the propensity for others to observe and assess the truth of that leadership. Such leadership examples are natural extensions of unique individual personality in situations where others need leadership to see their own future.

It's just as important to realize that leadership is lost when a leader fails to go in the desired direction of the followers or pushes others where they don't want to go. Leadership is also lost when a leader doesn't listen or is as blind to the truth as anyone else. Particularly, leadership is lost when the leader doesn't deliver on expected outcomes.

For example this applies in political life when a new candidate is elected to replace an old one who didn't deliver on promises. Teenagers reject parental leadership when the parent doesn't walk their own talk. Trust and team confidence can be lost by the head of a technology company who is unable to cause software development to become financially viable. Or a sales manager finds it hard to motivate sales employees to follow his or her lead when they're not achieving sales results.

Not delivering or underachieving on expected outcomes will have others cease to listen, question more, get diverted easily, or ignore a person who claims leadership while not being a leader.

Leadership is understood by the potential followers' perceptions of leadership, by the influence of role models, and by the leader recognizing aspects of a situation and responding as an effective leader. By considering all of these, individuals derive an individual leadership context.

2.0 PARADIGM

2.1 Recognizing Paradigm

Being alert, listening for, and recognizing paradigms, one can realize potential for extraordinary leadership.

I'm going to use this word "paradigm" quite a lot. This is what I mean by it: A paradigm is like a view of the world. It's how you recognize something and relate to it in association with an **already existing context** of what you think you already "know" about similar events from the past.

All human beings relate to new experiences from a background of their own personal context. It's like operating from a personal reference database. What many people don't know, or sometimes don't want to know, is you can alter this habitual reference base by consciously choosing to think something new in response to a repeated event or stimuli.

This is how it works. A situation occurs. Automatically the human mind begins to process what is going on. Unconscious questions are asked:

- Am I comfortable or familiar with what's going on?
- Does it fit with what I already know?
- Do I trust what's going on?
- Shall I automatically respond the way I always do when this happens?
- Or, is this a new experience? What do I do?

- Do I feel comfortable enough with what's happening that I go with it?
- Am I willing to step into what seems unfamiliar/familiar territory?
- What is the pain I want to avoid?
- Do I want to shut down and 'blank' this experience and not react?
- What is the gain of moving into possibly unknown territory?
- What do I choose?
- How should I react?
- Is there another way to react which could be better for me?

No doubt you can recognize these responses. The question here is — "Does one respond the same way in a familiar situation?" "Does one recognize there is the possibility of a habitual response AND the choice of a new response to something which has happened before?" When a situation occurs, there is always the choice of a habitual response or a changed response. A paradigm, or point of view of life, which influences choice can remain habitual, or it can be dynamically changing.

Begin to recognize paradigms you hold about yourself and others. Exercise choice to continue to behave inside existing paradigms or change your paradigms and thus choose new behaviors.

Astute new behavior responses may be required to build new paradigms.

For example, new paradigms are required where leaders and managers in business urgently require a strategy to:

- turnaround business performance in the face of successful competition
- stem a deteriorating cash reserves situation
- provide an alternative source of inbound raw materials
- stem high employee turnover
- manage the business through redundancies and layoffs
- manage and implement new processes to meet legislative changes
- boost market demand for goods and services

Historical methodology and thinking has got you into the current situation.

A new thought paradigm is needed for a new sustainable future.

In other business situations, a consistently non-changing paradigm may be more appropriate. For example, the historical leadership style of a boarding school headteacher can provide order and regularity. Leadership here can provide a stable environment for pupils to study diligently. Effective leadership that works here could be to 'get back to basics', the tried and true! Or management of a power generation plan which relies on utter consistency of practices to maintain electricity output and safety.

How appropriately you exercise awareness and the subsequent choice of paradigms impacts strongly on the quality of your leadership.

Remember - extraordinary leadership exercises the qualities of:

SELF-KNOWLEDGE – RESPONSIBILITY – COMMITMENT

2.2 Paradigm Example

Often you don't recognize the paradigm which has you mentally in its grip. **If you can't see different angles of the conundrum, you are likely to be stuck in an old paradigm.**

A way to recognize whether you are in the grip of an old paradigm of thinking is to think about looking at a colored rubber ball. The ball has two halves of different colors. Two people look at it from opposite ends of a room. Each would see the color facing them. If you asked each person to look at the ball and say what they see, they both might say "a colored ball". They both believe they are looking at the same thing. Each commits a different image and experience to memory which influences their paradigm of "colored ball".

If you then ask what color the ball is, one might say "a red colored ball". The other might say "a green colored ball". They are both looking at the same ball – seeing what they see – *what's available to their view* from their end of the room. Neither of them is aware that the ball has different segments of color. They both see a colored rubber ball from different angles, viewpoints, perspectives, or paradigms. Different meanings of imaginative construction are given to the same thing.

If you asked two people with existing antagonistic points of view *and* they each believed theirs was only *one* right answer, can you see that it would be difficult to agree on what was the "right" colored ball? Unless they're willing to look at the situation from a new context, thus observing the ball has different angles, and thus different paradigms of color can be perceived, they could be "stuck" with a fixed paradigm, or point of view.

WE ALL HAVE THE EXPERIENCE AT DIFFERENT TIMES

OF BEING STUCK IN A PARADIGM

NOT KNOWING WE'RE STUCK

YOU'RE STUCK WHEN YOU CAN'T SEE YOU'RE STUCK

An example of being in a stuck paradigm was how I listened to stories about apartheid when I was younger. Apartheid was a political system which physically separated black, colored, and white people in daily life in South Africa. When I listened to my school teacher, *I unconsciously created a context of apartheid.* I put into my memory a belief that apartheid was the permanent way of life in South Africa. I didn't question this thought. I was unaware I'd created this paradigm.

The moment, years later, I realized this untrue unconscious belief I stopped it, and my old paradigm was gone. I was open to a new way of thinking more capable of causing what I really wanted. Apartheid is **not** "a fact" that can exist forever.

People sometimes believe situations are permanent. The truth is they only exist by social belief and agreement. For example, The Berlin Wall separating East and West Germany was accepted for 28 years as a permanent construction. When enough people changed their thinking, the wall was broken down. Today, for example, the world accepts arbitrary borders for Israel, West Bank, and Gaza Strip imposed by superior military powers supporting inequality, segregation, and discrimination.

According to UNICEF, 22,000 children die every day due to poverty. The world accepts poverty as normal. The richest twenty percent of the world's population enjoy, and control, three-quarters of world income. The poorest forty percent accounts for 5 percent of global income. A sobering thought. The causes of poverty continue because those who can change their poverty paradigm continue in some way to accept poverty as an everyday fact of life.

Very few things in existence are forever. *Anything* **is** *possible* and **this** is the truth.

The apartheid political system in South Africa, for example, was abolished through a series of negotiations, culminating in democratic elections in 1994. New policies were chosen by the majority.

What paradigm of your own have you now uncovered from this discourse to improve a situation, which you realize you had accepted because you hadn't thought about it like this before?

Leadership makes the difference and causes the change. Effective and inspiring leadership works for a different point of view to be heard.

Being captured by a fixed paradigm prevents an open listening to others and stops a new reality occurring.

When you think you're taking affirmative action, no amount of 'doing' or 'taking action' will make a difference if you believe in something which is at odds with the goal of the action.

If you're taking a lot of action about something and not a lot is changing, it's hard work. Action in these circumstances is a struggle and you're up against it. Consider that the statement "I'm making a difference" doesn't in itself make a difference. **Results don't lie**.

Actions and your inner way of being must be aligned to words. A good hard look at the outcomes of actions reveals the truth. Results show us when words and actions unconsciously lack commitment and integrity. Non-alignment shows up. Results indicate the truth **when words pretend a belief and you just don't know it.**

WHAT THE OUTCOMES ARE TELLING YOU
– IS THE ACCESS TO TRUTH

I'll tell you a story about apartheid to demonstrate my point.

New Zealand's national rugby team, the *All Blacks*, proposed a rugby tour in New Zealand for them to play against South Africa's national team, the *Springboks*. The *Springboks* were an all-white team. At the time, there was no possibility of colored or black South African people being selected to play internationally in the *Springboks* team.

The *All Blacks*, a multicultural rugby team chosen on individual merit, represent New Zealand where laws and social behavior do not allow deliberate discrimination on racial grounds.

As a New Zealander, I decided if I did nothing to oppose the *Springboks* tour, I wouldn't be supporting the laws of my own country. Allowing tours to go ahead on an apartheid basis seemed to me to be passive agreement with apartheid. I decided to take political action and risked my personal safety in public marches to stand for multicultural policies.

At the time, New Zealand people were very strongly divided on this issue. Police presence was high and public unrest was the most marked anyone had ever seen. Police set up barricades arming themselves with riot gear, tear gas, and armored vehicles. Public violence erupted over this issue on an unprecedented scale.

Many people were doggedly determined to play rugby with whomever they wanted. They viewed interference as political interference in sport. Whole families were split down the middle and became very passionate about their stand on whatever side they were on. It was like a war. Instead we could have been inspired and motivated about peace and freedom between all peoples.

Just to relieve the suspense for you, I'll explain what ended this 'war'. A public rugby match was held between the *All Blacks* and the *Springboks* in Hamilton, New Zealand. Protesters against apartheid in sport (named HALT – Halt All Racist Tours) surrounded the rugby grounds. By sheer force of numbers, the HALT crowd overcame police barricades and broke into the rugby grounds. Protestors flowed onto the pitch (sports ground) in front of an audience of 70,000 rugby supporters.

A small plane overhead managed to evade authorities and dropped flour bombs on the pitch ruining it for play. These events were broadcast to rugby fans all around the world by live television coverage. The match was unable to get underway and the rest of the tour was called off. International television viewers, especially the white population of South Africa, got to see for the first time the strength of opposition to apartheid.

An official *All Blacks* rugby team was unable to tour South Africa to play the *Springboks*. It became impossible politically. There was no official tour until after the end of South African apartheid.

For many years, I thought I'd made a difference protesting "against apartheid". I realized later I was accepting apartheid as "a fact". I was "protesting" and "defending" multicultural society in New Zealand and "resisting" apartheid.

It was Nelson Mandela and the ANC (African National Congress) who showed effective leadership here. They focused the world towards a dream of co-existence between all people, thus successfully leading South Africa to a new multicultural society in South Africa.

Leading from a closed paradigm of resistance, criticism or denial doesn't change anything and it's hard work.

All the churning in the world is not going to move the wheels forward into a new dimension unless we can see clearly through the paradigm windscreen and get movement towards the future we want. **When you see where you're headed, it's easy to steer directly to the stated goal.** What your mind, words, and actions focus upon, and what you give time and attention to, is where you'll end up.

2.3 Leadership Paradigm

© http://www.dreamstime.com/Huhulin_info

Consider again the definitions of leadership such as leading and guiding others. Leading by being in front of or directing the movements of others. Leading by conducting another person by hand or by your behavior or guiding others by using persuasion. Leadership by guiding and influencing the actions or opinions of others. Leadership by causing others or leading others astray. Having leadership as a result or something. Leadership having first place in a situation such as acting as leading counsel. Leadership by enticing others to go farther than was intended by them or you or forming preparation for action. Leading by acting to introduce something new. Leading by directing conversation towards something, or taking a leading place.

You can see then in the context of leadership <u>when the leader is stuck</u> <u>in *perpetuation of an unhelpful paradigm, followers will also be "stuck"*.</u> *Leadership is the source for the group.*

WHERE THE LEADER GOES

OTHERS FOLLOW.

IF THE LEADER IS IN A STUCK PARADIGM,

TEAM MEMBERS WILL ALSO BE IN A STUCK PARADIGM

IF THEY FOLLOW THIS LEADERSHIP.

LEADERS HAVE A RESPONSIBILITY

TO EXERCISE

AWARENESS AND VISION

Look at how successful you are and how easy it is to achieve that success to indicate whether you are free of an unhelpful leadership paradigm.

We all unconsciously form paradigms and listen to others from within a paradigm context. We absorb "facts" to add to an already constructed paradigm and enlarge the picture of our "knowledge".

A paradigm is literally a point of view created from past information received, and individually interpreted to be stored with your own meaning. The meaning is whatever you choose. When a new experience adds to an existing paradigm, you are likely to continually build your context around this belief. You then selectively apply "meaning" to anything else you experience which you think fits with this paradigm or context of "facts".

Is this true?

There are a myriad of interpretations (like the possible range of colors one could paint on a ball) which can be created about any given situation. You see what you see and you don't see everything. You interpret every situation usually without realizing it. Clearly facts collected in this way are not true.

When a paradigm of stuck thinking or lack of results shows up, it's worth considering that "our problems are man-made therefore they may be solved by man. And man can be as big as he wants. No problem of human destiny is beyond human beings." John F. Kennedy

An important key to being a great leader is to choose paradigms or contexts for leadership which cause the outcomes or results you want to generate. Whether you choose a winning paradigm consciously or unconsciously doesn't matter.

A winning paradigm is one which allows for the truly desired future and the outcomes you say you want. Think about it. If the way you think (and the way you add more evidence to your paradigm point of view) is negative, do you honestly think anything positive or successful is going to happen?

2.4 Apollo 13: A Leadership Paradigm Example

The now famous words "Houston, we have a problem" were spoken by astronaut Jim Lovell aboard a space capsule 200,000 miles from Earth. A mission starting out to land men on the moon suddenly changed focus to returning the 3-man crew safely to Earth following an explosion on board. When the Apollo 13 command module failed, the crew moved to the lunar module as a lifeboat.

By a leadership paradigm shift, the mission then changed from accepting the problem of an unsuccessful mission to the moon to "failure is not an option". A shift in focus occurred from alarm and hopelessness to solution solving until successful shuttle return.

Anyone can register alarm in a critical situation which appears unable to be saved. Apollo 13 demonstrates how a desperate situation which appears to be an imminent failure can be turned around by utter commitment to success – even in the direst circumstances. Everyone focused on turnaround.

From such an inspiring leadership paradigm, a team was strongly inspired to forfeit counter-beliefs and utterly focus together. This caused the Apollo 13 mission to return to Earth successfully despite the odds. Possibility of success became inherent in every action.

Along with inspiration and focus, it is equally critical to utterly commit to the outcome declaration. To live "failure is not an option" is to live every thought, word, and deed, and to lead from that context. Success is a direct result of thoughts and actions within such a powerful context.

Remember - extraordinary leadership exercises the qualities of:

SELF-KNOWLEDGE – RESPONSIBILITY – COMMITMENT

To improve the possibility of a certain outcome, consciously choose a leadership paradigm capable of being cause of such a future. This is the way to be a successful leader.

2.5 Barriers to Successful Paradigms

Successful developments and strategies can occur when people give up fixed thinking, or thinking the way they did in the past. Business experience and business training alone doesn't provide wise thinking. It's worth pondering on these next statements to consider whether one's living fixed in the past or being open-minded to a new future. If you want to move forward on where you find yourself right now, and if things are not changing, consider whether one of these statements possibly applies to you. If it does, realize it, and change your thinking now.

"It is impossible for a man to learn what he thinks he already knows".[2]

"The eye sees only what the mind is prepared to comprehend".[3]

"The trouble with most people is that they think with their hopes, or fears, or wishes, rather than with their minds."[4]

"He who will not reason is a bigot; he who cannot is a fool; and he who dares not is a slave."[5]

---

2 Epictetus.
3 Henri Bergson.
4 Will Durant.
5 William Drummond.

"If we value independence, and if we are disturbed by the growing conformity of knowledge, of values, of attitudes, which our present system induces, then we may wish to set up conditions of learning which make for uniqueness, for self-direction, and for self-initiated learning."[6]

---

6 Carl Rogers.

2.6 Choosing a Successful Leadership Paradigm

You can choose a successful leadership paradigm by being prepared to re-examine something by looking at it more closely than you have before. It means being prepared to look *beyond* what you've been looking at up to now. It means being prepared to look *deeper*; to be prepared to *admit* things you might have resisted admitting before. We often don't see what we don't want to see and ignore what doesn't please us. In this way, we can be "inventing" facts.

To begin to recognize paradigms, first look to what you've created. To start to see, you look at what's around you. The structures and outcomes of your actions are all around you. Many are measurable or clearly visible and give indications on how you're doing. Some are not so visible and still need to be recognized and understood. By re-examining areas of your life, it's possible to notice what you didn't notice before, or didn't *want* to notice previously. There is no wrong or right here. We notice what we notice when we notice it. It's impossible to notice everything all the time. So don't make yourself wrong about it.

Many things are not as visible as other things and can only be stumbled upon when you're prepared to look more closely. One big "ah ha" can lead to another. Becoming aware of behavior patterns and outcomes is often as subtle as perception. Being willing to perceive your fellows as integral human beings with lives which affect them outside of your sphere enhances your leadership and their quality of life. Being willing to think outside of the box and beyond convention can open up an awareness of environmental impact which is essential to leave a world behind you one day for others to enjoy.

A simple example of the variety of paradigms people can create in business is provided by considering the buying and selling of melon fruit. For example:

A melon seller sets out with 20 melons to sell each day. He/she may sell all the melons each day at $10 each, *making $200 consistently every day*. At first perusal, this seller could conclude he/she is successful. Selling all the stock each day is a measure of success and creates cash in the hand. *What is the paradigm that cash represents to this melon seller?*

Looking closer, you might find the melon seller is also a melon grower. He/she contributes labor and costs to grow the melons him-/herself at a production cost of $7 each. Selling them then at $10 might still seem a successful paradigm, leaving $60 net cash each day. However, by the time living costs at $60 a day are deducted, there is *no accumulated capital and profits*. Nor does this business paradigm maximize the cash generating opportunity.

The melon seller could *change strategy* and *sell all the melons in one hour* each morning before other vendors have time to set up shop. If he/she then pays other people to grow his/her melons and keeps costs to $8/melon, only $40/day is made, but the rest of the time is available to sell someone else's melons for say $300/day. In this way, after $60 direct costs, the melon seller might generate a measure of real success at $280 a day. Success might then be measured in *improving profit margins* rather than cash revenues minus costs.

If the melon seller sold melons in an area well known for cheap bargains, he/she may sell everything for $200. However, if he/she looked again at the strategy taken, the same costs may be incurred, but *$400 can be made by selling them in a different locatio*n. This would **double cash revenues and double profit margins**. This is clearly a more successful paradigm of success to have in this situation.

Units	Sales price	Sales Income	Production Costs	Personal Living	Maximizing Time Earnings	Declared Profit
20	10	200	Not incl	Not incl	0	200
20	10	200	140	Not incl	0	60
20	10	200	140	60	0	0
20	10	200	160	60	300	280
20	20	400	160	60	300	480

Each seller sells 20 melons – different paradigms - different results.

If the melon grower knows there are other options, and he/she continues to sell with the same strategy, *and* is **satisfied** with the results whatever the sales takings are, then this is a successful paradigm. In this situation, if someone doesn't know what's possible and is dissatisfied, a change of strategy from a different paradigm would clearly be more profitable.

© http://www.dreamstime.com/Kacpura_info

One can be confined to thinking with the old historical approach of "sales price - resource cost= profit" as the only daily purpose. Alternatively, the melon grower might think outside of the box. Then the melon grower would recognize further hidden opportunities:

- recycled compost from others' waste to fertilize the melons
- recycled waste water from others to water the melons
- saving the melon seeds to plant new crop next year
- distinguishing the niche brand from competition by organic practices
- exchanging melons with neighbors in return for help on the land plot
- making hemp bags for customers to carry melon shopping
- re-investing profits to make hemp carry bags for all melon growers
- re-investing profits to buy transportation vehicle for melon business
- re-investing profits to buy transportation vehicle fleet to rent to others
- donating melons to local school to raise this melon brand awareness
- grading melons for different uses and different prices

- sponsoring an athletic team to raise melon business branding
- donating profit share to local college to help workers' family's futures

If someone is paying you to make a certain return and you minimize the opportunity rather than maximizing it, you are responsible for what you don't generate by being blind to a more successful paradigm.

Sometimes under-performers being paid by you are responsible for the less than expected outcomes. As a leader, you have the opportunity to lead your employees or team players to a more successful outcome by the way you lead the team. In this sense, "all" the responsibility for lack of performance does not lie with the employee.

Results are worth reviewing continually. The aspects of results change. At the end of the day, results are about meeting **your own** declared goals which can be re-declared at any time. Money as a goal is not everything and yet it goes a long way towards causing satisfaction for you and the people who follow you. Effective leadership is about being true to yourself and being true to whatever meets your criteria of success.

Leadership success is about fully using your unique natural born abilities and talents to experience all the possibilities you're capable of. Leadership success also contributes to others maximizing their self potential. Your success comes from your listening for others and your inspiration as you perform as a leader. For anyone, leader or not, full natural self-expression brings contentment and satisfaction.

For many, life is a struggle with little understanding and knowledge of how to replace the struggle with something better. Many people don't know how. Moving from struggle occurs by the willingness to admit a lack of knowledge of how to begin afresh and to make the right choice to change. The possibility of leadership is discovering the ability to show others the way to their success.

A SUCCESSFUL PARADIGM

IS LIKE BEAUTY

IT'S IN THE EYE OF THE BEHOLDER

EVERYONE'S IDEA OF SUCCESS

IS DIFFERENT

CREATE A PARADIGM

WHICH MEETS YOUR NEEDS

If the melon grower for example doesn't know about another paradigm *and* he is a dissatisfied or unfulfilled person, it would be worthwhile for him to assess his fixed paradigm for the possibility of changing it. His old paradigm will be stopping his business from expanding, changing, and being able to maximize sales income from the resources available. The change he needs to understand and make, in order to realize the possibilities he is capable of living, may relate to melon growing, or may go beyond melon growing, for him to get satisfaction from his life.

However, money is not the sole measure of success. While the melon grower may make profits, he may still be dissatisfied by the sullen or non-communicative attitude of his workers paid the minimum wage while struggling on the breadline. The melon grower may want his children to enjoy the company of local children. He may realize he needs to share profits so that other families can enjoy more abundance and their children are happy. His child will benefit socially from his ability to uplift the well-being of the community.

He may also realize he can reduce traffic and air pollution to his community by better using local natural resources for melon fertilization or packaging. This procurement strategy may not show a profit or be easily measured; however it's a hidden benefit which has long-term impacts for a sustainable community life.

A business defined as a legal corporation is an organ of people who communicate in order to trade resources. Business doesn't have the right to destroy the environment from which it sources resources to trade. Nor does business truly have social support to destroy any environment. Leadership of business which is not sustainable is not sustainable successful leadership. Sustainable business leadership must consider more than the one dimensional short-term profit and loss and balance sheet aspects when making corporate decisions.

There are many possible scenarios on the melon grower example. This may seem like a trite example, however, if you look at any given situation from the perspective of possible new angles, there are always more alternatives to be found. It's only an old worn out paradigm which keeps us blind. No matter how sophisticated a situation may seem and no matter what the previous context of knowledge, capability, resource, or responsibility might have been, there is always more to learn.

One doesn't stop looking until the desired outcomes start to show up as a reality.
How do **you** know whether you're successful? You know you're successful when you're being truly content, happy, satisfied, fulfilled, and not desirous of anything else but enjoying each moment – AND – other people are enjoying the same in a sustainable way. If this level of contentment in each moment is not present, then it's time to start wiping the fog off the windscreen and see where and why you're steering off track.

Start questioning how it's going.

IF YOU START TO REACT AGAINST A SITUATION

YOU KNOW IT'S TIME

TO LOOK AT

THE PARADIGM YOU'RE RUNNING ABOUT IT

Consider for example whether you're running any of these paradigms:

Other people are going to take care of me:
"Expecting the world to treat you fairly because you are a good person, is a little like expecting the bull not to attack you because you're a vegetarian."[7]

Everything in life is always hard work:
"If it's hard, you're doing it the wrong way."[8]

I'm a hard worker and deserving of high pay because I work long hours:
"Being busy doesn't always mean real work. The object of all work is production or accomplishment and to either of these ends there must be forethought, system, planning, intelligence, and honest purpose, as well as perspiration. Seeming to do is not doing."[9]

How can anyone fault me? I am always so efficient:
"There is nothing so useless as doing efficiently that which should not be done at all."[10]

I work hard at my job. I can't figure out why the business doesn't do better:

---

7 Dennis Wholey.
8 Penny Whiting, sailing professional, and recognized author on *The Americas Cup*, http://www.pennywhiting.co.nz/index.php.
9 Winston Churchill.
10 Peter F. Drucker.

"If one does not know to which port one is sailing, no wind is favorable."[11]

I work hard. It's not my fault I'm not as successful as others are:
"You have to learn the rules of the game. And then you have to play better than anyone else."[12]

---

11 Seneca.
12 Albert Einstein.

2.7 Assessing a Situation - Warts and All

To know how something is truly going, the questions are:

- What are the visible results?
- Are the visible results acceptable to you?

Ask yourself these questions and write down your answers.

Talk to trusted colleagues, independent advisors, industry experts, mentors. See if someone else has observations to add to yours.

To become more successful, look at the facts in operation reports, financial reports, progress reports, program management timeline measures, for example. Think of questions about the factual results to uncover new observations, and new ways of looking at things you've not been aware of, especially to uncover information not stated in reports. Reports are not the final and complete answer. Reports are indicators of aspects which warrant further investigation. When you've had a first pass over the results, and you've come to some conclusions, ask yourself questions like these for example. You may discover the true drivers of your results:

- Are these visible and invisible reports and conclusions acceptable to you AND everyone else who is involved?
- Do the results represent a true picture of who you think you

are as a leader, or what you think your organization is? If not, what are you proposing to do about it?

- Are you living the words you say to people, and what you say to the media?
- If you say you want to be happy, are you mired in conflict?
- Are other people around you mired in conflict?
- Is there back-biting and gossip going on?
- If you want to grow an enterprise, do the published results show consistent year on year growth? If not, why not? What can you do differently in future to ensure year on year growth?
- If you say you're profitable, are you increasing your profitability margin percentages, or are you simply increasing sales with the same profit margin?
- What were the underlying drivers of earnings/profits in the past? Are these drivers going to change? What are you going to do to change tack and make sure there are drivers of success for you in the future?
- Do you consider you have a successful company when you have the highest staff turnover in the business?
- Is the 5 year projection reliable when most of the growth is dependent on the growth of one key customer or one area of historical business growth? How much control do you have over these projections for example?
- Are other players in the industry expanding their market share at 15% while you sit at 3%? What does this comparative trend tell you about your business? What's behind the variance?
- Are you aware of how others are doing? How knowledgeable are you?
- What is your reaction to competitors' progress? Are you happy with this?
- Are you making record profits and leaving a wasteland behind you?
- Are you exploiting your team without creating leadership succession?
- Have you considered everything, or are you presenting only

what you want to make visible to appease yourself, or to look
good to others?

Be open to expand your vision. Seek to recognize what is holding you
back from a full range of choices in your situation. Reflect on habits
of human behavior as follows to help you reflect and discover what's
really available:

*"Often we say we describe what we want, and think we have it. **WHAT
WE SEE DEPENDS MAINLY ON WHAT WE LOOK FOR.**"[13]*

"Often we read the world wrong and say that it deceives us."[14]

*"In this world, there is nothing softer or thinner than water. But to compel
the hard and unyielding, it has no equal. That the weak overcomes the
strong, that the hard gives way to the gentle. This everyone knows. Yet
no one asks accordingly."[15]*

*"Every man takes the limits of his own field of vision, for the limits of
the world..."[16]*

The first thing to recognize is **how** you're looking:

- Are you looking at the results subjectively or objectively?
- What is the underlying influence or constriction to speaking
  the truth?
- Can you say the truth in the face of fear of rejection?
- Can you listen to other peoples' points of view and take them
  in?
- Can you face your fears and do it anyway?
- Does it matter more to you what others think than your own
  truth?
- Are you capable of being fully responsible?
- What are the areas you need to work on?

---

13 John Lubbock (emphasis added).
14 Rabindranath Tagore.
15 Lao-Tse.
16 Arthur Schopenhauer.

QUESTION YOUR ACTIONS. TO LIVE INSIDE A SUCCESSFUL PARADIGM, YOU START BY LOOKING AT RESULTS OF YOUR ACTIONS.
What actions move you towards what you say you want? What actions don't move you towards the desired outcomes? If what you say is going to happen, but what happens doesn't tally with your promise, take a look at the paradigm from which you operate. Clearly you've been kidding yourself that this was possible coming from the paradigm you're in. It's time to take a long hard look at your paradigm; consider updating it.

You might now be saying: "I already know that but I don't know what I'm doing wrong!" First of all there is nothing wrong. What is, is, that's all it is.

I know that if you'd known, you wouldn't still be doing it. Would you? I know you're not stupid. Keep looking for keys to success. You'll see it if you keep looking.

2.8 Aspects to Consider

Here are some examples which may provide clues to understanding why a situation is not generating the results you want.

2.8.1 Attitude

If you're not getting the desired result, look at 'how' you're doing it. Before "doing" something have a look at your *attitude*. Are you making requests of staff or in a relationship where you're being rude, offhand, brusque, callously demanding, angry, or superior?

No matter how much others are paid, and no matter what the material rewards you may give, others are not likely to respond well when you make a request with "attitude". The exception to the rule is super generous attitude people who are able to rise above rudeness and brusqueness.

To change an attitude which isn't working for you, consider reading "Change Your Mind - Change Your Life": "*Most of us want to change the world, but only a few of us are willing to change our own minds!*"[17]

17 Gerald Jampolsky, *Change Your Mind - Change Your Life* (ISBN-10: 0553373196; ISBN-13: 978-0553373196).

THE KEY TO SUCCESSFUL LEADERSHIP

IS NEVER 'OUT THERE'

IT'S WITH YOU!

You may not see the pathway forward at first – we often don't. Don't make the mistake of finding someone or something to "blame". This just takes us into denial and dumps negativity into the situation.

If you can't understand what to do, or don't know a solution, remember that Rome wasn't built in a day. Give yourself time. Let yourself be until new ideas present themselves to your mind. In time, an idea will come to you leading to a breakthrough in your thinking. Have patience with an open mind.

Do what you know to do and wait for inspiration for the rest.

Know what you want and hold onto that idea. Keep the focus.

2.8.2 Predictable Outcomes

Are you repeatedly getting unsatisfactory outcomes? Then wake up.

If you keep repeating a habitual approach or methodology, the same outcome will keep on turning up like a bent penny. Why wouldn't it? You haven't changed tack! If you want something different, reset your sails.

Learn to manage behavioral issues by handling your own behavior.

Start with being honest with yourself about what it is that you're doing or not doing which is contributing to a lack of leadership or leadership difficulties.

When you can recognize what's not working, find an appropriate person to admit and acknowledge your unhelpful behavior. Find a way to give up what's not working and create the space to bring in a new beginning. Communicate that new beginning clearly and bring it into existence with others powerfully.

Organizational change is managed by managing the organization of your own behavior.

©Alicia Yao, M-J Howe

Access to seeing where to change your behavior is always found in the results you generate.

The first step in seeing how to change is to be willing to change. That didn't work – so what's next? Stop talking, pushing, and dominating with attention seeking behavior. "Be with" what's so and get to know every aspect of the problem or situation you're hating. Don't run away from it.

The new direction will turn up by continuing to hold an open mind and not trying to impose or dominate a situation with your "old" solutions.

2.8.3 Incomplete Communication

If you want someone to communicate with you, or you want them to deliver something to you, it's your responsibility to ask them to acknowledge your request. It's your responsibility to seek confirmation of acceptance of the request. You 'own' the request until they take action and grant that request. Your attitude, actions, and implicit expectations will have a significant impact on the outcome of your request.

If you request a delivery, it's your responsibility at the outset to state *how* and *when* you want the request delivered in order to establish the parameters for a successful outcome.

If you want to be an effective leader and you accept responsibility to deliver service to meet someone else's expectations, you want to be operating with this same conciseness too. What do they want precisely, by when, where, and for what consideration?

It's poor leadership and incomplete communication if you say you'll take on a commitment and:

- forget
- don't deliver
- don't deliver everything you said you would
- don't deliver and ignore repeated requests for delivery
- pass it off to someone else who doesn't comply
- deliver instead what wasn't asked for and agreed to
- lie because you have no intention of delivering the request
- over commit yourself elsewhere and then use this as an 'excuse'
- change your mind
- consider "it's not important" after all

Successful leaders are specific about commitments, accountability, and arrangements.

For example, to arrange a conversation time successfully, make a request. Have the other person agree a time and date which works for both parties. This starts you on the right foot to successfully getting your request met.

Rather than launching into a conversation, 'trying' to have a conversation, or feeling ignored because someone always seems to be 'busy', by making a request for a future time conversation you have taken a step in positive leadership.

By getting agreement to converse, a shared responsibility is created and a willingness by the requested recipient to participate. This places a bridge between two parties making the first steps in communication easier.

This is in contrast to not considering whether your request is convenient to the other party or riding oafishly over their lives by directing or ordering the other to do what you want. This approach lacking mutual agreement puts up barriers between people and closes off avenues to successful outcomes.

When avenues of communication have been damaged by previous behavior, there is an incomplete communication. The term 'mending bridges' applies to situations where one needs to recreate a willingness to communicate or contract with another when mutual agreement was not previously obtained.

How people react is their own interpretation. Common sense tells you there are ways you can behave to generate co-operation and positive listening.

Weigh up how truthful you are about your leadership goals? If you truly believe you can lead a situation to your stated goals, give up beliefs and behaviors which lead away from this goal.

A successful leader is constantly acting in alignment with goals, such that resulting facts confirm the plan's viability.

For example, did the communication **work**? If it was incomplete, take on the fact that successful leadership is about your performance – not the other persons.

If you want results, look at the part **you** played in the outcome. Your part in what happened is the only performance you have the power to change. If your communication or action didn't get you want you wanted, be positive about it, and towards the other person. Establish the facts of what really happened. Start again with a more successful attempt learned from what worked and what didn't work the first time. Choose to modify your approach for more success next time.

2.8.4 Thinking It Through

Prepare for what you want. Think about the resources you have and how to use them to best effect.

If you want a Chief Financial Officer (CFO) to deliver an *upbeat report* on sales financial results to a management meeting, how do you make sure it happens?

Past experience may suggest your CFO presents reports with lots of numbers in a quiet mumbling voice. You've observed this causes employees to stop listening to vital information. They seem to hear it as boring. The CFO's presentation doesn't occur for them with clarity or relevance to the audience and yet you know it's vitally important they listen and remember the information content. The content has key information which should cause your employees to modify their behavior and company systems for the business to be successful.

As Managing Director (MD), what do you do?

- Do you sit back and let the CFO continue knowing the communication style is likely to be unsatisfactory and unchanged?
- Do you say nothing, while thinking to yourself: "Am I being so stupid that I can't get this person to do better?"
- Do you throw your hands up and think *any* CFO dealing with numbers can't be expected to do any better?
- Do you wish *you* could do it better, but you don't have the time?
- Do you become generally critical, isolated, and uncomfortable with the CFO, feeling somehow you are to blame, and yet "they" are not delivering the communication the team needs?
- Do you just write off your thoughts with "he/she's an idiot" or "he/she's a fool"?
- Do you wipe your hands of it and complain to others about the person?

OR do you exercise responsible and inspiring leadership, and quietly suggest setting up a **new** format to the CFO and offer to work with him/her on it?

- Do you ask the CFO to report to you with a preview of a new format?
- Ask him/her to highlight areas they consider important for notice by the management team?
- Have conversations on likely ways to interest the management audience?
- Do you establish *what* messages the CFO wants audience to be left with?
- What would have the audience be more interested in the financial results?
- How could reports be presented to cause the management team to take action in their own area by being better informed of the financial impact of their actions on the overall company results?
- Do you ask the CFO if he/she can understand what style of information and presentation might get the target audience more interested and what the CFO might propose in order to meet this need in the next presentation?
- Is your feedback honest about what you agree with/don't agree with?
- Do you decide on a communication strategy collectively and specifically ask the CFO to prepare by an earlier date and time in order to review with you before the presentation?
- Do you ask the CFO if he/she has any concerns about that request and work with them to resolve those concerns?
- Do you ensure the CFO is quite clear about what you want and is capable and supported to do that?
- Do you provide training and support the CFO to such a level that you can guarantee that the communication from the CFO at the next management meeting is going to make a difference to the understanding of everyone who hears the communication?
- Do you focus on the measurable results this 'CFO makeover' will achieve?

- Do you delegate or take over in communications with the CFO?
- Will you be relaxed leading the next meeting knowing your homework will guarantee maximum positive impact of group communications?
- Is your leadership style sufficiently authoritative for you and others to trust that new issues can be handled with thoroughness and professionalism?
- Do you notice people are open and willing to offer contributory ideas?
- Do you create forums for their ideas to be considered by you and others?
- Do you observe management team members being respectful towards you as they see the standard of preparation, consideration, and professionalism you apply to every area of business at hand?
- If not, why not? Take time to really consider this train of thought.

When you think about it, taking the time to assess what wasn't working and creating an effective plan to work with members in your team so they can be successful – GUARANTEES – that you will be successful as a leader.

In the example given above, taking leadership responsibility to ensure the results you want is bound to generate a CFO communication style which hits the mark and is more likely to cause the group results you want. It may seem like hand-holding at first, and it may not seem like your job. However, if you don't want the results you've already had, don't continue with hands off. Successful leadership is:

SELF-KNOWLEDGE – RESPONSIBILITY – COMMITMENT

DO WHATEVER IT TAKES!

2.9 Others Follow Your Leadership Paradigm

Consider the Apollo 13 leadership paradigm of "failure isn't an option". The team leadership faced up to reality very fast and dealt with it even in the face of possible utter failure. Such a leadership response was so inspiring that it was followed not only by the space shuttle crew and the base team in Houston. It was later followed by organizations worldwide.

If you're experiencing failure right now, I invite you too to consider taking up the leadership motto of "failure isn't an option, we will succeed!" The route you are on may not look like the route to success you imagined right now. However, with your focus and determination to succeed almost any route can be successful in the end.

If you don't have commitment to success, you get failure.

Consider again the launch of Apollo 13 and compare this for example, to Western governments' leadership of public health relating to the dangers of cigarette smoking. Those who could have acted for many years took an ostrich type approach to leadership responsibilities. Some even suppressed official advice so it could be ignored by them and others. They carried on with commitment to outdated thinking.

Instead of acting promptly on overwhelming evidence of harm to health, public health leadership resisted banning cigarette smoking in public for years. While resistance went on, aspects of the truth about tobacco smoking were perceived by the public from a blinded and uninformed paradigm.

The public relied on health professionals and public leaders with health and science qualifications and professional standing in the community to be custodians of public health. The change in leadership came eventually by legislation. It was a long time coming.

When you hold an official position, you have a greater responsibility in leadership. People follow not only you. They also follow the office you hold.

LEADERS

ARE FOLLOWED

WHEREVER THEY LEAD.

PEOPLE

CAN BE LED

TO

THEIR SUCCESS

OR

TO THEIR DEMISE

Leadership is about raising the game. If it weren't, we might as well be sheep.

Followers listen selectively to what a leader has to say and try to relate it to something which matches their already existing paradigm.

If people believe you *ought* to know more than they do because they see you as better qualified as an official to give an opinion, they will likely place more reliance and trust in your advice or believe *your* opinion is more valid than their own. In these leadership situations, you have a duty in law and a moral duty to take extra care from a position of advantage. In other words, your leadership has a fiduciary duty.

3.0 FINDING YOUR INNER LEADER

3.1 Going inside the Walls

Sometimes a leader lives inside a paradigm with *thin* walls by being open minded to new ideas and concepts. Thin walled leadership might be described as open, engaging, approachable, sometimes radical, or innovative. It also includes being prepared to be challenged or willing to collectively challenge new ideas, notions, or proposals. The possibility of thin walled leadership is high when one is able to recognize and acknowledge existing paradigms from the past with an attitude of openness. This presents an ability to consciously construct changing paradigms from which to work.

In everyday leadership, it can be said the skill and awareness of openness to perceiving now what wasn't obvious before, is the access to very powerful leadership. Being an open listener and observer illuminates new avenues in communication and is more likely to cause events to turn out differently from historical trends.

By contrast, one can live leadership inside a paradigm with *thick* walls – resistant to any chink of change of consciousness. Thick walled leadership can just as easily attract followers and can also be the source of powerful leadership. This thick walled leadership is more likely to cause a predetermined outcome because the possibility for variation from what's been done before is low. Such a leadership paradigm can be appropriate for captaining a ship or airplane in ordinary circumstances, where consistent methodology and interpretation of events is critical to the safety and successful operations of the crew.

Successful paradigms of leadership are about meeting required needs. Leadership more resistant or less likely to change is very appropriate sometimes. Alternatively, leadership open to listening and creating new product ideas on a continual basis can be essential to survival in a competitive sales market, for example.

Leadership is successful when there's effective communication giving the greatest opportunity to others to have their needs met and thereby having your needs met.

For example, being successful as a product development or marketing manager is not adding new product features and components to production and expanding marketing campaigns just because you can. It's about ascertaining customer needs or creating customer needs and matching them.

Successful product development and marketing leadership correctly perceives customer problems and successfully meets them with the right solutions. Success is achieved by a communication of the benefits on offer such that the customer sees those benefits as the solution to their problem and *wants* the benefits offered at a purchase price representing benefit to buyer and seller.

It's important to keep questioning whether you're hitting the mark with leadership goals. If you aren't succeeding, consider what Albert Einstein once said "We can't solve problems by using the same kind of thinking we used when we created them."

The past has given us wonderful experiences and has taught us much. And the past is the past. It's over. The world keeps changing and we need to adapt and change with it. Don't you want to live today and respond to the unique circumstances of **today**?

"This is the way we've always done it" is an appeal to tradition which is a logical fallacy. Leadership from the past is just that – it's leadership from the past. It only fits in the present if it fits the present needs.

Thick walled paradigms can work if we're aware of them. Be aware and consciously choose a particular paradigm of leadership to suit the occasion. If thick walled paradigms are not appropriate and we are struggling with shifting them, we could consider breaking down the walls with something soft.

3.2 Walls Illusion

You create all the thoughts you have in your mind. You can easily choose to un-think those thoughts and replace them with something else. You were born with a clean slate without any thoughts in your head. From birth, you have built a huge library of thoughts which make up the truth as you see it today.

Paradigms are all made up. You can make up more as you go along. You'll get to enjoy them and have mastery over your life if you recognize the paradigms by which you live. Learn to distinguish paradigms.

I'm going to show you a variety of ways you can spot your old paradigms about your own person - and invent some new ones.

3.3 The Paradigm of Who We Are

You create and believe a paradigm of yourself which limits who you are. Is this paradigm the truth of who you are? The answer is a resounding NO!

This is an opportunity to look at who you think you are. While doing the following exercises, you may find yourself mentally saying two different things to yourself. You may agree with an observation and at the same time question it. Some people could explain this as a feeling of having a little voice inside your head saying the opposite of what you want to think. This is sometimes described as what your internal dialogue is saying. What your internal dialogue is saying is NOT who you are. It's just a voice. Let the little voice sit on the sideline for a while for this exercise and don't believe all it says. Be objective to the opposing inner voice during this exercise if you can.

CONSCIOUSLY SUPERVISE YOUR OWN MENTAL CHATTER

The leadership exercises which follow are not meant to be done perfectly first time. This is not about doing things perfectly.

You will get the most out of this study by reading it several times and doing the exercises for yourself many times on different occasions. Each time you do the exercises, your life will be in a different situation and you'll see things differently. The more you look at the areas suggested here, the more you'll recognize and be able to convert thoughts and actions towards the reality you really want.

This study is intended to stimulate increased awareness of how to uncover what's hidden in the morass of daily life.

Who you really are is the one experiencing leadership in your life. What you perceive as truth is not the truth of what's going on. You're not as in charge as you think you are.

I want you to reach a point where you re-think thoughts regularly each day. A point where you think: "Where did I get that idea from? Whatever had me think that? Is this true?" Then choose to wind the tape back and re-think your response to what just happened. Consciously choose your response in the next circumstance. Consciously create the life you want and create the way you want to be in the life you create. This is true mastery of leadership.

The answers are all in the mirror of your life. If you can see in the mirror, you can see more clearly what's really going on!

3.4 Looking into the Mirror

Consider you're like a polished, smooth mirror surface reflecting images. You're a looking glass. What you see outside you is the reflection of what's inside you. Everything in you is what's reflecting back at you. You are the cause and the reaction to everything that's around you. That's who you are as a leader.

WHAT'S WITHIN – IS WITHOUT

Consider you're reflecting yourself outwards. Whether you're aware of this or not, this idea might just be true.

If you choose, you can live as if other people's opinions about you matter and let those opinions define who you are for yourself. You could also choose to meet other peoples' ideas of who you are under the pressure of what, in their opinion, you *ought* to be.

Or you could live in a way to create the outcomes **you** choose. Living this way, continually modify your behavior to create the reality **you** want "out there". If you keep looking in the mirror of life by observing how people respond to you, you'll see the reflection of your life like a mirror. You can take this reflection as a reality check of what you're creating. Compare what you think you're creating and what you are creating by seeing what's in front of your nose.

Another leadership coach might suggest that the classical synopsis of this kind of leadership presentation includes the importance of personal appearance. You might get advice on how to dress, how to walk, how to impress others with who you are. My approach is not about that.

When you're being a leader, other people's opinions don't determine what you do or how you are. Other people's opinions and reactions can sometimes be good feedback, like a reflection in your mirror of what you might be projecting from within yourself unconsciously and not be aware of it. This you can change if you want a different result. Other times, other people's opinions can be nothing to do with you at all. Other people will think what they think and they don't have to change for you to be a powerful leader.

Recognizing the mirror of life reflection is a powerful leadership tool and a reliable way to cause successful leadership. It's a reflection of something. It doesn't define who you are. If you change your style of leadership, the whole situation will change regardless of what clothes you wear.

Smart clothes, powerful body language, and accessories do impact others. Beyond the outer clothing, you'll only be a truly influential leader by being perceptive beyond surface level appearances.

3.5 Smokey Mirrors

Do you ever notice that you keep repeating frustrating experiences, failure, tragedy, trying too hard, dissatisfaction with emptiness, being late, being disorganized, unable to communicate easily with others, working long hours, not making progress when you want to, or not impressing the people you want to impress? Consider all such outside experiences are a reflection of something within yourself.

I describe the mirror as smoky because you're looking at something you can't yet see. How to see it is to look and look deeply. Don't take any half measures in seeking to see. Look until you're just blown away with what you've never noticed before.

3.6 Discover Message in the Mirror

3.6.1 Bare facts

Do **the Bare facts exercise (a full page print size exercise is available in Appendix 1)**

Start by looking at yourself in a physical mirror. Look really hard.

- Who do you see?
- What does it feel like?
- What is the emotion you see there in your eyes?
- What do clothes communicate about how YOU feel about yourself?
- What is your body revealed communicating to you?
- How do you feel about posing to yourself?
- Do you know how you posture your body in company?
- Where were hands, arms, shoulders, legs in company? And now?
- What are you saying in body language?
- What do you think other people see when they look at you?

No, I'm not talking about the look you give yourself in the mirror as you run out the door, or flash past the company bathroom to check your tie's on straight, hair done, teeth cleaned, and for ladies, lipstick and make-up is intact.

I'm talking about taking quiet time by yourself and really looking. Looking into the eyes of the person you haven't seen for ages. What do you realize immediately?

Have you said hello to *you* anytime over the last 10 or 20 years? Or has that time *with* yourself *for* yourself just rushed by? Now is a good time to say hello and get familiar again. You're going on a journey and you need to know who you're talking to if you want to cause yourself to be a great leader.

Consider who you are for *yourself*. Your internal unspoken conversation is visible and almost palpable in your presence and is displayed by what you surround yourself with. Even when you're not aware of it, others experience your self beliefs. These are the beliefs you know about as well as those hidden from your consciousness. The unspoken part of your conversation often comes across more clearly and powerfully than spoken words.

To direct and master life opportunities to cause your goals, you need to discover the person you project to others.

Leadership will be an empty communication process if you're operating like an empty robot. If you're empty of connectedness and self-awareness, other empty people will gravitate toward you. It's true "birds of a feather flock together". Like does attract like. If I have a lot of robot like people following my leadership who are empty of self-awareness, there's not much chance of me, or them, being motivated, excited, and inspired by my leadership. Instead I'll be experiencing not making much of a difference. You can imagine the kind of results this is likely to generate.

3.6.2 Posture/Bare Appearance

Do the Posture/Bare Appearance exercise (a full page print size exercise is available in Appendix 2)
To make a difference, it's not what you look like that counts. *It's who you think you are that counts.* Who you think you are is reflected back to you not only in the bathroom mirror but by your success or lack thereof as a leader. At first when you look in the mirror, you don't really know who you are. This makes for a bit of the blind leading the blind, don't you think? Check it out!

You may think you're well-dressed and you may think you come across a certain way to others. But look further than that and look at how you and others respond to you. Are you in touch with reality? Or are you living with your body and being oblivious of its feel and appearance because you're stuck in an old or artificial paradigm?

You will see reality pop up when you consider questions like these:

- Do people's eyes light up when you arrive and they see you and what you're wearing?
- When you're out with others who you consider to be superlatively well dressed and presented, do you notice if they are completely at ease with you – or not?
- Do you find yourself being self-conscious of something about your appearance all the time? For example, your stomach pokes through your shirt buttons, your hair is going bald, your neck hairline needs tidying up, your glasses are old and old fashioned, your shoes need replacing or cleaning, your fingernails are bitten or dirty, your jowls are bulging over your shirt collar, your teeth are not looking healthy, you've got hair in places you don't want it, you've got acne, you can't get comfortable with your sore back, or you don't even notice your shoulders all day until you lie down at night and they're screaming with pain from being bunched up all day ?
- Do you notice that your bag, your shoes, your suit, your glasses, your wallet are all a mishmash of styles and colors and you feel "cheap"?

- Do you have impeccable clothes but you sweat easily from nervousness?
- Do you feel nervous being around others who are not as well presented as you?
- Are you the one who puts on bravado to cover up what's not obvious to the public? At home, your life is chaos and out of control
- Are you the one who puts on social bravado and your bank statements are well colored with red figures?
- Are you always trying to give the impression you're not committed to anything or anyone so you don't miss out on something else?
- Do you notice people you admire are completely comfortable being near you physically, or do they keep their distance?
- Do you wonder if you've got body odor or bad breath?
- Do you feel commanding as long as people keep on the other side of the room and nothing remotely personal is said?
- Do you dread going into certain situations like a party, a board meeting, the office, public relations cocktail events, the school gala?
- Are there particular clothes you are more - or less - comfortable with?
- Do you suffer from "can't be bothered!"? Do you ridicule yourself or other people, thinking you're past it or who cares anyway?
- Are you listening, but not really listening, thinking this is all about "other people", it doesn't really apply to you?
- Does an old memory of what someone said to you come to mind, something you've not remembered for years?
- Do you want what you see, or do you despise it?
- Do you feel sad, happy, curious, or paralyzed with fear?
- Do you feel excited or confronted to be taking time out for you instead of for everyone else?

You might take a good long look in the mirror at your appearance and see what there is to see.

It's not about comparing yourself with an unrealistic model of superman or a skinny model; it's about being with yourself. It's about wearing clothes which acknowledge who you really are. It's about addressing any physical aspect which has you be uncomfortable.

Accept what you see. This is you. If there's anything you're particularly uncomfortable with, forgive yourself for being critical and judgmental. If there's something you want to change, and can change, such as toning up muscle, then <u>list what to do, how, by when. Stick to your list and do it</u>.

When you can love yourself the way you are, and the way you're not, you're being conscious and alive with who you are. When you're at home with yourself, comfortable in your own skin, others are consciously at home with you too. Being this way adds power to anything you say or do as a leader.

3.6.3 *Mirror Me and My Soul*

Do you feel completely natural and relaxed with anyone else? Do you sense that others feel completely relaxed with all aspects of you?

If you answered "NO" to this last question, some soul mirror work will work wonders.

When I first really looked into the mirror deeply, the way I hadn't in years and years, I went from being a fairly self-confident individual to being someone who realized I'd been "away" from my body and myself for years. I realized my clothes were "stuck" somewhere years ago when life became a bit overwhelming and I'd left myself behind there somewhere. What I was presenting physically to the world had nothing to do with who I thought I was in my head.

As I kept looking into the person in the mirror, I found I did like the person into whose I eyes I gazed. The pleasure of my friendship was unable to be dented by anything anyone else might say about me. I felt my feet on rock solid ground. This was a moment of clarity!

A fashion designer friend indicated he'd like to "give me a makeover" and I went shopping with him with a new lease of life. You might say this is what women do. It's true: some women 'do shopping'. This was different. It wasn't shopping to buy 'something to wear'. It was shopping to be myself, listen to advice, observe what clothes truly reflected externally how I felt on the inside.

With a new wardrobe fitting, the person inside the exercise released me to be authentically who I am inside and out. The next time I looked in the mirror, I recognized the person reflected there. The person I think and feel that I am is out there on display fully participating in everything.

Ever notice how people who are 100% authentic get heard?

I can't recommend enough looking in the mirror in this way to see who you really are today. Check out the mirror regularly to see the truth reflected back to you! If you need to take action as I did, do it.

3.6.4 *What Is in the Mirror?*

Do the Mirror exercise (a full page print size exercise is available in Appendix 3)

It's your turn now to look in the mirror and visit there. Be your own best friend. Go look in the mirror!

Give yourself an uninterrupted quiet 30 or 60 minutes to look and be with yourself. Relax and go away into your own mental space. Imagine you're introducing yourself to someone you've never met before and see whether you want to know them. See what you discover. <u>Please write down what you notice in subheadings as demonstrated below</u>

(print the list below (in expanded form in Appendix 3) and write 2-10 lines about each question. Date it and keep it. You'll no doubt do this exercise more than once. It's good value to see the difference over time.)

Date it. Keep it.

Questions:

What I saw of myself at first glance.
What I saw of myself in the clothes I wear to represent myself.
What I didn't see of myself in the clothes I wear to represent myself.
What I saw of myself when I went butt naked in the mirror – front and back.
What I saw when I looked into my own eyes and said hello – who is there?
How long is it since I really looked at myself and said hello?
What does that feel like?
What does my hairstyle/haircut/hair color/lack of hair represent, or doesn't represent who I am and how I really feel inside?
What am I saying to others by my appearance?
What does my face and neck represent to me?
What do my hands represent to me?
What do my legs represent to me?
What does any other part of my body which comes to mind represent to me?
When I am dressed at home – how do I feel in my body?
When I am dressed socially – how do I feel in my body?
When I am dressed doing exercise – how do I feel in my body?
When I am dressed at work – how do I feel in my body?
When I am dressed or undressed on a beach – how do I feel in my body?
When I am standing in front of an audience – how do I feel about my body?

What is the part of my appearance I am comfortable with?
What is the part of my appearance I am uncomfortable with?
What do I like/dislike about my physical features?
What do I like/dislike about my hair?
What do I like/dislike about my teeth?
What do I like/dislike about my face?
My shirts?
My jackets?
The color of my clothes?
The cut of my clothes?
My shoes?
My jewelry?
My trousers?
My skirt?
My stockings?
My socks?
My tie?
My casual clothes?
My dress up evening clothes?
My work clothes?
My accessories?
My travel bag?
My briefcase?
My watch?
My jewelry?
My hairstyle?
My makeup?/skin tone?/skin color?/pallor?
My deodorant?
My perfume?/aftershave?
My belts?
My coats?
My hats?
My scarves?
My gloves/mittens?
My swimwear?
My golf accessories?
My tennis accessories?
Other?

Anything else?

3.6.5 My Mirror Impressions

Now have a look at the list you've created in the appendix. Do you see some strong reactions or impressions of yourself you didn't realize before?

It could be overall that you are neat as a pin but boring.
It could be you're disheveled and needing a good spruce up.
It could be you look good but you aren't happy.
It could be it's an overall good look, and you now realize the "capable" look is actually a big cover-up because you're worrying.
It could be your whole appearance needs work, but there's potential there.
It could be you suddenly realize you're not so bad looking after all.

Whatever you see...
Write it down... keep the list... you'll want to refer to it again later.

3.7 Health

Do the Health exercise (a full page print size exercise is available in Appendix 4)

Successful leadership requires vision and an execution plan. An execution plan won't work if there are unsorted obstacles in the way. Start by cleaning up your own act. If you're carrying around the burden of unsorted health issues this will sooner or later affect your physical, emotional, and mental abilities. This will affect you and the people who rely on you.

Oftentimes, when you clean up an area neglected for a long time you notice other opportunities to clean up in other areas. Taking time to look at your state of health is likely to remind you of something you've been ignoring for a long time. If you ignore a health area which needs attending, it'll eventually show up as a major problem and can defeat you at the finest hour of leadership. So = do it now! Take a good hard look at your state of health.

THERE IS NOTHING WORSE THAN BEING 'ALMOST' SUCCESSFUL

Other people are more likely to enroll in following someone reliable, fit and healthy. You'll notice as you progress to becoming more physically reliable, fit and healthy, other exterior aspects of your life will also become more reliable, fit and healthy figuratively speaking. Reinvent your leadership ability by knowing your own state of health and looking after yourself.

Write down health problems that you know of, or are worried about. Write down the daily habitual actions you take which you know jeopardize your health such as:

- smoking
- drinking heavily
- taking drugs
- unprotected casual sex
- sleep deprivation
- overeating
- not drinking enough water
- listening to negative people
- not enough exercise
- poor diet

Write down actions you don't take which you often think about such as:

- walking
- going to the gym
- sport
- more rest and recreation
- more social time to relax
- receiving massages
- taking vitamins
- listening to music
- relaxing with your children
- dinner by candlelight with your spouse or partner

Your body is like a well-oiled machine. If you leave it out to rust or give it the wrong oil, it'll seize up. Consider what you're doing to your body on a daily basis. Does this nourish you?

Work at giving yourself the full and complete answers to the questions here. There's nothing to get stressed about. Give yourself time to do this valuable exercise. Write it all down. Create your own worksheet so you can re-do the exercise from time to time, and track your change progress.

Facts are just that – facts. There is no shame in facing facts. They're what they are. There's nothing to be gained by ignoring facts or denying the truth. If you deny the truth, the only person you're really hurting is you. So just accept yourself: the good, the bad, and the ugly.

- What do you see about your state of health?
- Have health problems been going on for a long time?
- Are there aspects of health which need attention not procrastination?
- Do you trust your body to be strong and powerful to support you in an expanded and powerful experience of leadership?

Do you notice some areas of your body, health, or appearance you haven't attended to for years?

Attention to detail and replenishing in all areas leads to optimum leadership performance.

3.7.1 The State of Health You Want

Many times when we look at health, we unconsciously assume standards of health that we think are inherited from our families. Or we may have accepted standards of health and physical well-being similar to people with whom we work or socialize. These may not be optimal states of health.

"Your health is bound to be affected if day after day you say the opposite of what you feel, if you grovel before what you dislike, and rejoice at what brings you nothing but misfortune..."[18]

---

18 From Boris Pasternak, *Dr Zhivago*.

It's not easy to imagine yourself as something other than the way you've been for a long time. When the tone pectorals (pecs) or slim arms and legs of youth morph into 'blobby', many people 'tune out' to body deterioration over time and bunker down to indulgent living. However far you've gone off track, it's always possible to get back onto a track to improved health.

If you're already super fit, improvement could be to arrange more relaxed and unstressed activities to give your body and state of mind time to repair and revitalize.

If you're overweight, and everyone around you is overweight, your body plan review may signal you aren't happy to accept this state of health for you.

Turn towards other people who've mastered the aspect of health you desire. Observe how their daily patterns differ from yours and see if you can learn from and apply these different styles of body activity to your own life.

Ask for the help of professionals or read a book on healthy living. What's important is to see who you are and what you are, and get clear on who you want to be. Create a plan to become the person you want to be. If you have a goal and you begin down a path towards it, you may not know all the answers to get there now, but you'll learn by being prepared to start from a beginning now.

Your body may be functioning and yet it's sluggish and far from top form. Consider reading good books on the subject of health to recognize your situation and get some ideas on how to get well again. For example:

- Adrenal Fatigue The 21st Century Stress Syndrome by James L. Wilson
- 8 Weeks to Women's Wellness by Dr Marianne Marchese
- Food Combining For Health by Doris Grant and Jean Joice
- Juice Fasting & Detoxification by Steve Meyerowitz
- Creative Health Beginning The Journey To Wellness by Dr Andrew Bell

You could also consider kicking into action with a fast action detox program. I went to Astumi Healing Center in Phuket, Thailand for several weeks. On another occasion, I detoxed with www.ploughshares.co.uk in England. There are many good detox centers. Investigate different offerings. Choose one which intuitively feels right for you. Many people do a detox program at a center annually to keep themselves in top form. There are also good mini—detox programs for purchase online, such as www.blessedherbs.com, if you don't have time to spend two weeks out of circulation.

If your health problem is an alcohol problem, speak to someone who listens without judgment. Start by admitting the true state of affairs. Feel the shame, pain, the fear of being out of control, the anguish, the worry, or the pretend bravado about your life with alcohol. Admit it. Decide you want something else for your future. Create a plan to have that happen. You could start by attending Alcoholics Anonymous.

If you haven't had good sex for a while and you've just woken your repressed sexual needs by reading this book, start to imagine how good sex would be if you were enjoying sex: the way you know you could with a body shape which gives you confidence, and being able to express normal enjoyable sexual feelings. Start by acknowledging to yourself your lack of satisfaction. Write it down if that helps. Find an appropriate person to share your thoughts about your sex life without making sex an overly significant issue. You may want to share with your partner that you'd like more sex or you'd like sex a different way. Don't expect others to meet your every need just because you want it. Look at why you're sexually frustrated. Is it because you can't communicate? Is your body out of energy for sex? Or are you trying to get sex and going about it the wrong way. You may want to find a good sexual counselor to improve this area of your life.

You may want to find someone who cares about you enough to hear you say aloud your feelings of lack of self worth from lack of sexual activity or sexual satisfaction. As you open up about your emotional and physical feelings, you may realize not enough sex, or not enough sex of the kind you want, is impacting on you. Not being sexually active may cause you to abandon feelings of self-worth in the bedroom and in other areas of your life. It's time to improve overall feelings of self-worth. You need to feel self-worth, self-confidence, and be able to trust others to be an effective leader.

Alternatively, you may be a sex addict or be behaving illegally sexually. You can consider admitting your sexual problem and be willing to acknowledge the health, emotional, and reputation risks to you and others. In the beginning we are all born perfect. We develop behaviors through life experiences. Nothing that shaped you going in this negative way is "your fault". However, as an adult, you are now responsible for your behavior. You'll pay a price if you carry on behaving with negative impact on others.

If you've a beer gut or tummy paunch, a simple start to moving fat overload and toxins is body massage. A body massage might be a new experience. With an experienced professional masseur, a massage can be at once an exhausting experience and at the same time invigorating. Stress is released and circulation improved. Massage can be a reminder of how good your body felt in the past when it was more in action with healthy exercise.

Love yourself and determine to enjoy life more. Consider taking up a new sport. Start by taking long walks in the countryside at the weekends and move that fat. Avoid fast food stops and instead take a brown bag lunch and vow to avoid 'second helpings', deserts, and alcohol until you get the weight down. Anything which is a jump start to the new life you want will propel you towards the state of health you want.

You may have a bad heart or heart palpitations and need a complete rest. You may have episodes of gout or have varicose veins. There's a need for care and medical support to keep on top of chronic conditions. Love yourself and realize only you can take time out for you because you're worth it.

From the exercise of examining your health, you may decide there's a part of your body you don't like. You decide it's something which, if you had time, money, or commitment, you'd do something about it.

For example, to improve health and self-esteem, you might want to attend to:

- enlarged nose or broken nose
- acne
- bitten fingernails
- bunions
- cellulite
- chest hair
- crooked teeth
- dandruff
- double/triple chin
- ears which stick out too far or actual big ears
- facial hair
- halitosis
- kidney stones
- lack of muscle tone
- protruding stomach
- receding hairline
- size
- skinny arms
- thread veins, broken veins, spider veins
- ugly glasses

3.7.2 Body Health Check

Do **the Body Health Check exercise (a full page print size exercise is available in Appendix 4)**

Write down observations of areas of health, body, and appearance. Anything you think needs attention. Keep writing until you can't think of any more areas. (There's a checklist in the Appendix for you to complete)

3.7.3 Body Plan Checklist

Your body and your own person are a living organism. Can you imagine how much growth and fruit you'd get from a plant if you never watered it?

If you want your body to support you, support your body. Supporting your body means notice it, look at it, listen to it, care for it, nurture and be conscious of how it's feeling. Your body is comprised of cell tissue and water. Like any living organism of cell tissue and water, your body will wilt if you don't feed it with enough pure water. It'll grow weak and floppy if it's fed toxins. It'll wilt and die an early death from lack of care.

Did you ever see a stunning leader who was a weak and floppy person? Did you ever see a leader who lacked invigoration being very inspiring? Your energy needs to be clean and clear for you to reinvent leadership and cause the kind of results possible.

This doesn't mean you can't be a leader if you're paraplegic or born with a crooked eye for example. Energized people are people in a frame of mind to do something. They are making the best of the talents God gave them.

If you look after the body you're born with, it'll be able to look after you. When you can look after yourself well, you're well equipped to perform a stewardship role for others in leadership. To a reinvented leader, a body ignored will be an underutilized asset at best and a liability at worst.

3.7.4 Benefits I Want

To reach for something more than the present situation, people need a desire. If it's never occurred to you to have a better shaped body, consider it *is* possible to have the healthy and energized body you want.

Anything you want to become is possible. The only thing between you and a dream is to invent a dream and take action to cause the dream to become reality. To realize a dream, hold that dream in your mind. Every day do everything you know to do well towards realizing that dream. This way what you dream, you will realize.

Who are your role models? What do you admire in others? Find out what your role models or heroes did to become who they became? Is their path relevant to your dream? I don't mean dreaming vacuously about magazine cover models. I mean observing habits of role models whose achievements inspire you and whose example has you believe your dream is possible too.

Arnold Schwarzenegger (Arnie) is proof that everybody with a dream and perseverance can realize their dream. Arnie decided to capture the *Mr. Universe* title. To prepare, he needed to workout in a gym. When Arnie first walked into a gym he was literally awed, however the membership costs were too high for him. So he equipped his own gym in the basement of his parent's home.

Arnie won his first contest in spite of not having the vaguest idea about how to pose. That first success officially started his bodybuilding career.

In the process of preparing to contest and win the *Mr. Universe* title, Arnie met a mentor and started training with him. He claims he learned a lot from him, such as how to better train the parts of his physique which were more in need of development. Most importantly, he learned how to improve himself as a human being.

Arnie first promised himself he'd exercise his body to become *Mr. Universe*. Then he stated this to others. Whenever Arnold lost a contest, he knew something was still amiss in his training. He eventually learned **how to think to win**. As he had promised, he triumphed.

To think he was capable of winning was nothing to do with how anyone else performed. Arnie learned to **think of himself as a winner**, thus overcoming the final hurdle of psychological intimidation by his opponents and reaching his dream.[19]

If you want to become a winner, you have to go through the process:

- **Invent a dream**
- **Prepare and take action - small beginnings lead to great things**
- **Enjoy and celebrate small wins**
- **Learn by your mistakes - prepare and try again**
- **Expand input resources**
- **Focus on niche areas of development**
- **Create measurable objectives (MO)**
- **Communicate MO to others**
- **Do what you say**
- **Overcome obstacles**
- **Think yourself a winner**
- **Be a winner**

Write down what you want *your* body to be. State what you're prepared to do to have this body. State quantitative measures you can use to know when you have become the body you want to be.

---

19 See, for example, http://en.wikipedia.org/wiki/Arnold_Schwarzenegger and http://www.bodybuildinguniverse.com/arnold.htm.

3.7.5 Mind Talking to the Body

"If you realized how powerful your thoughts are, you would never think another negative thought. Thoughts can be a powerful influence for good when they're on the positive side, and they can, and do, make you physically ill when they're on the negative side."[20]

Mind talk is another name for self talk. It's the mental conversations you have with yourself. A conversation either in your head or aloud. These "conversations" can be self-critical or be positive and supportive.

To create a positive body image requires positive mind talk. Your body deserves to be treated well. As you become consistent with treating your body well as a result of your thoughts, you'll notice a difference in how you feel about yourself.

Research into the effects of mind talk concludes that what people say to themselves even affects their ability to combat and ward off illnesses.

---

20 Peace Pilgrim. From 1953 to 1981, a silver haired woman calling herself only "Peace Pilgrim" walked more than 25,000 miles on a personal pilgrimage for peace. Her message was both simple and profound. "If you realized how powerful your thoughts are you would never think a negative thought. They can be a powerful influence for good when they're on the positive side, and they can and do make you physically ill when they're on the negative side." Excerpts taken from http://www.peacepilgrim.com/steps1.htm. A documentary about an extraordinary woman, Mildred Norman, includes interviews with Dalai Lama, Maya Angelou, John Robbins, Elizabeth Kubler Ross, and newsreel footage from 1950s, 1960s, and 1970s, on her walk for peace (http://www.spiritual-happiness.com/video.html); Documentary Film, "Peace Pilgrim: An American Sage Who Walked Her Talk" (http://www.peacepilgrim.org/FoPP/index.html).

"A positive mental attitude as a basis for self-talk doesn't require self-delusion."[21] It's in your power to transform your body image by the way you think. If you want to reinvent yourself as a leader, think yourself into a strong and healthy body to keep you strong, allowing you to enjoy life to the maximum.

"Change your mind – change your life"[22]

Mind talk will have you become a great leader with a good body image. For example, here is some "mind talk":

I am who I am. I am unique and there will never be anyone like me again. I am on a *unique* life path which unfolds with enjoyment, prosperity and success every day in every way.

I and my *accomplishments* are worthy. I love the things I do well and I accept the things I am improving. I feel good about myself.

Wow, I am worth *compliments*. I feel good with compliments. Compliments give me the warm fuzzies. I am thankful for being appreciated.

Keep calm – enjoy! I have the power to let myself think anything I want to think. I am powerful. I choose to think....

---

21 "A positive mental attitude as a basis for self-talk does not require self-delusion. The development of optimistic thought patterns requires essentially three things: recognizing self-talk for what it is, dealing with negative messages, and harnessing the positive for the greater good of individual persons." (http://www.ericdigests.org/1994/self.htm) Solipsism is a philosophical theory that everything is in the imagination, and there is no reality outside one's own mind. See http://www.youtube.com/watch?v=LMzbwa6PvEE and http://www.youtube.com/watch?v=rHXXTCc-IVg.
22 Gerald Jampolsky, *Change Your Mind - Change Your Life* (ISBN-10: 0553373196; ISBN-13: 978-0553373196).

I look in the mirror every morning and enjoy looking. The parts of me I think are attractive remind me how I love myself anytime I want to. As I love myself with enthusiasm, I shine inwardly and outwardly.

The more I like myself, the easier it is to like other people. I am enjoying noticing attractive people more and more and giving them compliments.

I love myself. I choose to appreciate good aspects of myself. I love every cell in my body. I am worthy of being loved.

I'm happy with life. I can enjoy myself at (16) stone. I was born with a big frame and I love my body.

Or I love and accept myself, my short framed body, thin body, wide body, brown body, white body – any kind of body. I can take care of my body and love it to the best that it can be. The more I love myself, the more I receive loving.

I am conscious of the knowledge of "you are what you eat". I am satisfied with nutritious food and clean water. My body is strong and healthy.

I take care of my body; I feed my body good food that I truly enjoy. I am strengthened and revitalized. I taste my food and I honor my body by being aware of what I eat.

I love to exercise. I increase oxygen into my body by breathing deeply. I feel a tingling with energy and vitality.

I enjoy creating time alone to exercise. Alone time gives me quietness to contemplate and let go of stress from my mind. I am fit and refreshed.

I enjoy team sport. In team sport, I release tension and enjoy friendly banter with others. I am having fun, being invigorated and motivated.

I love sex. I am sexually attractive. I am worthy of enjoying a happy and satisfying sexual life.

I love what I wear. I feel like a million dollars in the clothing I wear. My wardrobe is amazing!

My body is designed to move. It is normal for me to walk, run, and dance. I move and connect with my body. I feel how incredible my body is. My body supports me in everything I want to do.

In this moment, I am alive, prosperous and satisfied. I love what I do and I'm being paid millions to be who I am right now.

Walking quietly in nature is therapeutic and comforting for me. I enjoy nature. Birds sing and the sun shines. I hear the song of nature exalting in joy.

I feel my breath. I see and hear my breath. I breathe slowly and deeply. Breath sustains me throughout the night when I sleep.

I breathe deeply during the day. I concentrate on breathing, quietly drawing oxygen into my body. I feel great as I breathe deeply and feed my body with oxygen. I am alive and revitalized.

4.0 BEING MORE SELF-AWARE

A body image review along with increased self-awareness is not a criticism or self-flagellation exercise. It's positive to acknowledge what you see and live with it. It's not right or wrong or inadequate. Nor is your body a manipulation tool for you or for others. Your body lives to support you to live your life well.

The next person you meet for the first time has no past with you. The future begins now. If you want a future with others different from the past, learn new skills today. You **can** cause a change from the past. Your experience of others will transform whenever you're ready to transform yourself.

After you've completed these exercises and taken a good look at yourself, you may consistently notice more about your environment and how people in it behave in a way you didn't see before. In this observer mode, notice how you respond. Are you becoming more aware of how you relate to others?

Being more aware, you may find yourself:

- sitting up straighter, slouching less
- pulling in your stomach
- easing your neck and shoulder muscles
- breathing deeply now and again
- looking in the mirror to say thank you to your body for supporting you

Enjoy the body appearance aspects you like and decide to love the rest. You may be motivated to get a new haircut, fix teeth, get a new razor, new makeup, clean your shoes, get a manicure, get new shirts to fit the true shape of your body, buy a bag to match a wardrobe item, ditch the flashy watch or ring, or take some more vitamins.

You may also notice a great person in the mirror whom you can love and cherish. You may see yourself for the first time as someone bursting to 'come out' and be noticed, appreciated and rewarded in the world. As you raise your self-worth, it may cause a desire to be treated well. From this new perspective, you may consciously take action to give up accepting second class treatment from others, or from someone in particular who is abusive. You may become more assertive with someone whose behavior upsets you and decide to stop shutting down emotions and giving up by 'accepting it'. Now you quietly and firmly request a change or move away.

You are worth the best. When you actively love and accept yourself, others will love and accept you. Love and accept yourself and you're more likely to treat others with respect. Treating others well is a hallmark of good leadership.

Many books explain how to raise your sense of inner worth, such as "You Can Heal Your Life" by Louise Hay. With a higher sense of self-worth, you're more likely to be compassionate, encouraging, straight, and respectful towards others. This makes for a much more attractive leader for others to follow.

You'll experience more happiness in every area of your life when you've reached a higher self-awareness. Keep working on it. Self-awareness is a fun area to work on constantly. Your life will change enormously over time for the better.

4.1 Body Messages

In a typical office, there are watchful eyes at every turn. Observe your body responses, and you'll improve your image, job prospects, and abilities to lead others. How you are within, with self-talk, will show on the outside. Here are some body language tips to think about while you're on your coffee break:

- Enter a room with openness and purpose. Walk in a brisk, easy stride with your eyes forward. Look around with ease. Hold your head up proudly with easy self-respect. Look around a room to show you care about your surroundings and to see who is present. Acknowledge others by looking them in the eye. Where appropriate greet each individual. Don't stride about too much while addressing people otherwise your body posture can be experienced as domineering, intimidating, or disrespectful to others. You want others to be *in* your world to be an effective leader, you don't want to repel them. Consciously communicate to be welcomed into *their* world and provide openings for them to be related to you. Listen openly without fear.
- Stand with weight balanced evenly on both feet with shoulders

back and arms relaxed. Avoid commando postures such as hands on hips (i.e. 'you can't tell me what to do') and hands clasped behind your back (i.e. 'I'm angry and fearless'). Stand calmly during a tricky phone call for example. Standing calmly will have you feel and sound empowered. The other person will sense you're open and listening to them with consideration.

- Respect people's personal space. For an average person, this is 60cm on either side of the body, 70cm in front and 40cm behind.
- Body mirroring is subtly mimicking the position and mannerisms of the person you're with. Body mirroring will make you appear like-minded and in agreement.
- A smile works wonders. A smile makes you appear approachable. There are two types of smiles:
  - The involuntary Duchenne smile[23] which works the muscles around the mouth and eyes and reflects genuine feelings.
  - The voluntary Pan American smile which has a forced 'have a nice day' feel that suggests insincerity. A smile that is too forced becomes a grimace.

Every look and gesture down to the twitch of an eyebrow communicates an inaudible message. Body language communication is just as important as verbal language in understanding emotions and intentions. Reading body movement communications correctly is often more effective and accurate than words.

The manner in which someone physically communicates can be a powerful indicator of how that person really feels.

There are different theories as to what movements indicate which feelings or intentions. The basic non-verbal communication perceptions are:

---

23 In physiology, a smile is a facial expression formed by flexing the muscles most notably near both ends of the mouth. The smile can be also around the eyes (Duchenne smile). Among humans, it is customarily an expression of pleasure, happiness, or amusement, but can also be an involuntary expression of anxiety, in which case it can be known as a grimace. There is much evidence that smiling is a normal reaction to certain stimuli and occurs regardless of culture. Happiness is most often the cause of a smile. See http://en.wikipedia.org/wiki/Smile.

- crossing of the arms and legs indicating defensive gesture (one either doesn't want to be bothered or is seeking sympathy)
- holding of the hands behind one's head indicating superiority
- shaking of arms, legs, hands or feet indicating stress
- fiddling with earlobes in males and playing with hair in females indicates attraction to the person being spoken to

4.2 Start with Yourself

To be an effective leader of others, you need to be an effective person. You need to be fully alive, aware, and in touch with the way you think and do things and the impact of that. So if you're not effective now, it's simple: Just wake up to who you are – the good, the bad, and the ugly! Move yourself to a better mental attitude along with a commitment plan to become effective.

Notice how your body automatically acts in different situations. Observe your feelings. Make active choices to change your thoughts at any time if this isn't how you want to be. Your body will reflect how you're feeling in a new awareness.

Create an action plan in your diary with dated commitments to actions. Address areas that woke up in the body exercise. Begin your action plan now! Make commitments and make sure you do them. Review the list each month. How did you go? What did you do? What didn't you do? Why?

Diarize your next date with the mirror. Have a pen and pad at the ready. State to yourself while looking into your eyes in the mirror:
"What I am going to see the next time I look here is ....
....
....
....!"

Make another written statement and describe the future you plan in detail as if you're **describing a picture to a blind, and deaf person who has no taste buds or sensory organs. Describe every picture, sound, sense, and feeling you can imagine about what you want to create as if you are creating from a blank slate**.

- Read aloud this statement of the future you're living into often. Often means at least daily
- Add more detail as you think of more you can envisage
- Believe now that you can have this future; know it's possible to have this
- Take the steps you know to do to have it become reality. As you take these steps, you create the path towards the goal. Keep taking more steps forward as the next steps occur to you. There is no need to push or worry.
- Let go of the rest, including worries or mental doubts. Keep focused on the future you say you want so as to attract the aspects of it which haven't yet happened.
- Believe the whole future you describe in detail is possible for you
- Take the time with inner focus to imagine this future every day
- When you're in planning mode, quietly work on it and don't tell other people what you are doing
- The more you create this, the more you're sowing the seeds of what's possible

Gradually, day-by-day, the change occurs. Before you know it, you ARE the person you truly know yourself capable of being. You draw the future to you that you truly want.

You've now created a new future of who will welcome you into the mirror in the future. Are you excited? If not, go back and do it again. Don't limit yourself. Doing this exercise, you've now created a new future of who you will welcome into the mirror in the future.

As you become more aware of how you respond and feel each day, you start to notice what other people are doing in a way you didn't notice before. By being aware, you have more conscious and positive behaviors plus communication style choices to influence others to follow your leadership. In this way, you create your life and your own leadership of it consciously.

The keys to successful leadership are:

SELF-KNOWLEDGE – RESPONSIBILITY – COMMITMENT

How you are with your body and how you conduct yourself will have a decisive impact on being able to be powerful and successful in leadership.

4.3 Cause Your Life the Way You Want It

You're responsible for what happens to your life. You're responsible for what you do and what you cause others to do. You're responsible for what you don't do and what you cause others not to do.

If you look at leadership from the perspective of being the one in the position to change things and no-one else can change your life for you, you'll start to sense how powerful you can be in your own life.

If you were to say you wanted to become a pharmacist, for example, it's entirely up to you to cause this. No-one can do it for you. You're the one to organize resources to enable you to study. You take the study and do it. You then demonstrate to others how you're qualified to practice as a pharmacist. When you've done that, a Governing Body of Pharmacists will give you a practice certification acknowledging the self-knowledge you demonstrate. When a certification body allows you an authorizing pharmacy practice because you reach the agreed knowledge and performance standards of the profession, you're ready to start business.

Having that practicing ticket doesn't get you to be a pharmacist by itself. It's your responsibility to market yourself to attract customers. At no point along the way can anyone else live your life potential for you.

If, in another example, you hold yourself out to be the manager of an organization. People rely on you to manage. They may not say so directly, but they will be looking to you for guidance and direction. To fulfill the potential of a management role, you need training and development. Create a plan to get it.

Any leader delivers guidance by written instructions or verbal directions in meetings or conversations. A leader mentors others. Most particularly, leadership occurs by being a person who acts towards others such that they perceive you as their leader.

If you aren't getting the results from others you think you should be getting, the nub of the problem is with you. Leadership is never about anyone else; it's all about you. Successfully achieving leadership is authentically being yourself and being competent in the role such that others relate to you as their leader.

My father was a naval leader during World War Two. He used to say "not on my watch". I consider this when I hold management leadership responsibility. I am responsible for what goes on and how it's handled. It's my job, not anyone else's, to ensure the team delivers on its promise. Everyone does their task to complete the job. Ensuring tasks are completed, and completed on time, is my job and an expression of my competencies. Leadership can only work successfully where responsibility is paramount.

5.0 INTEGRITY AND LEADERSHIP

5.1 What is Integrity?

Many people talk and write today about the need for integrity in leadership.

What is integrity? How do you know whether you have integrity?

Integrity is being what we appear to be. Integrity is being what any object or information appears and is stated to be.

A boat, for example, is an object which could not be a boat if it didn't float since floating makes it a boat. If a boat is leaking, it lacks integrity. If the rate of leaking becomes extreme, the boat will sink and become a sunken boat. A sunken boat is not a boat anymore. It becomes something else. It becomes a sunken boat or a wreck. A boat is not a boat unless it can float.

Relate this integrity concept to areas of your life.

5.1.1 Health

If you have a stomach ulcer, high blood pressure, a high cholesterol count, excess weight and a lack of fitness, does your body lack integrity? In this state, a body is out of integrity. In a poor or extreme state of ill health, a body is breaking down. If lack of integrity became more extreme, a body would become a corpse.

5.1.2 Mode of Transport

Does your car look edgy or flashy to impress others while inside the driver is feeling like a loser? Or do you drive a car without insurance or without a roadworthy certification? These are examples of a car and driver out of integrity.

The car without a roadworthy certification will likely fail mechanically and may cause the driver and passengers injury in an avoidable accident. The driver is risking being permanently unable to drive by losing a driver's license at law.

The car chosen for its image may be inappropriately mismatching the driver's authentic emotional state. It may not be driven very often if the owner is uncomfortable to live such a life of pretense. The car then becomes a display rather than being a vehicle. Does an article built to be a vehicle and not operating as a vehicle have integrity?

5.1.3 Business

Is your business maintaining a high turnover, but profits are sabotaged by grumpy staff interactions or staff rudeness to customers?

Do you undermine the business customer service image by having grubby premises?

Do you add extra charges at every stage of point of sale to trick people into paying extra once you know they want the product offering?

Here are some sure signs of business leadership out of integrity:

- Lack of pride by employees or premises appearance
- Lack of respect for others
- Poor interactions between staff
- Under-par business services presentation or grubby premises
- Messy incomplete transaction records
- Incompetent cash management
- Underperforming information systems
- Lack of security systems
- High levels of pilfering, excessive expenses claims
- High levels of sick leave
- Deliberate misrepresentations of products or service offerings
- Poor customer service
- Use of poor quality resources for production
- Slow payments to suppliers
- Destruction of or carelessness for environment by business operations
- Loss-making operations
- Downward trending business results
- Management doesn't act unless media or employees complain
- Extreme polarities between employee group remuneration levels
- False reporting

5.1.4 Relationships

People are often found in the company of others with similar values. Many choose to date, co-habit, contract marriage, and socialize with people of similar interests and values. Group values are signaled by behavior, conversation, physical dress, attitudes, and unspoken social agreements.

From this perspective, it is to be expected that a well-dressed person would feel uncomfortable walking out with a long-term relationship partner who looks like a frump. Such outward signs of divergent values can be a sign of relationship out of synch: one person indicating a high sense of self-worth and the other not. If you're in such a relationship, is there something untrue about the relationship you're both avoiding? Is the relationship serving the best purposes of each person? Is it a sustainable long term relationship which works successfully in your social grouping?

An old saying describes how people naturally group as "birds of a feather flock together". It would also be natural to discover similar patterns amongst people working together. In business, why would a business manager who presents himself and his business well hire sloppily dressed people with differing attitudes, morals, and conversation?

The more at ease people are with each other the more likely they are to get on and work as a team.

At work, why would you fail to commit to your own personal ethics and presentation, which properly represent who you are? If you have a social circle that fits, why would you lower your social satisfaction by committing to work:

- in sloppy business premises with people who don't care about how they present themselves?
- with thieving dishonest people when you're not a thief yourself?
- in a business which disrespects its employees or customers?

Check out the state of symmetry in your life. If you can recognize a lack of symmetry around you, consider making changes to create a more authentic grouping. As a leader, you may notice a need for improved symmetry with people you employ. Do some employees need to be moved on to a place which better fits them? Or you may be an employee who notices the leadership team doesn't behave in a way which fits your own values. Are you working at the right place? If the employees are not a well-functioning group, the business won't be a well-functioning business.

To further understand integrity, one may speak of the integrity of a wilderness region or an ecosystem, a computerized database, a defense system, a work of art, and more. When applying integrity tests to objects, integrity refers to the wholeness, intactness or purity of a thing. A wilderness region has integrity when it is not corrupted by development or the side-effects of development. A wilderness has integrity when it remains intact as wilderness. A database maintains its integrity when it remains uncorrupted by errors. A defense system has integrity as long as it's not breached.

Some ways of looking at integrity:

   i. integrity as the integration of self
  ii. integrity as maintenance of identity
 iii. integrity as standing for something
 iv. integrity as moral purpose
  v. integrity as virtue.

Integrity is not backing out of commitment. You are true to your word.

Integrity is when you don't say something to schmooze another person, or to make yourself look good in another person's eyes.

When a group behavior is common with others, and known by others to be wrong, and something prohibits you from inside yourself not to do the same as others do – this is also being in integrity.

5.1.5 State of Office

Is your filing cabinet a mess and tax returns not in on time? Are you paying inordinate amounts of avoidable interest by not managing daily cash flow better? Do you reply to correspondence promptly, or does it "go on the pile"? These are easy signs that the administration organization of business leadership is out of integrity.

A business office exists to 'do the business'. If it's not operating to 'do the business, it's out of integrity and it's not a business office. It's a dumping ground for paper, it's a pretense, it's a place of denial. Is your office a fortress guarded by minders titled Executive Assistants? Is it an office inaccessible to others without the right pass? What is your real perspective of team leadership while working in isolation creating the illusion of a power base? How connected are you to team members in the organisation, your stockholders, and customers? What sort of message do you think others have of your leadership? What do the business performance indicators tell you? While the office hub lacks aware, effective, and timely administration leadership, business performance goes down.

5.1.6 Personal Cash Management

Are you cash rich with overdue bills not paid? Sooner or later when bills aren't paid on time, the price of delay will be paid by you. Leadership is out of integrity if your behavior and attitude is to not play fair in this way.

Similarly, if you don't collect on receivables, leadership is out of integrity.

Being out of integrity has you:

- be less powerful in delivering your communication message
- suffer from reduced inner self-confidence
- be intuitively distrusted by others
- cause doubt in the minds of others about the integrity of what you say

Such a lack of personal integrity WILL show up in your performance measures if it hasn't already.

Deal with whatever needs to be dealt with and get back on track.

5.1.7 Public Image

Are you pretending to be successful and masterful and not being successful or masterful? Communication is out of integrity. How do you know if this is true? When people don't act on what you say, this is a sign of communication being out of integrity. People don't believe you.

As President Lincoln said, "You may fool all the people some of the time; you can even fool some of the people all the time; but you can't fool all of the people all the time"

Discover what is 'out' and put it right. Untrue aspects of communications or behavior have a habit of becoming more exaggerated in the public eye when they're not dealt with promptly.

5.1.8 Variety of Situations for Integrity

Integrity is an interesting subject. Integrity means different things to different people in different circumstances. If there is no pretense and you're getting the results you want, you probably have integrity.

To illustrate integrity, you could say leaving dirt on a car is out of integrity because layers of dirt will wear out the paint and reduce the value of the car. However as an example, if a car is dirty and unkempt on arrival from a long journey, it's in integrity because it's being used for it's true purpose of travel. Cleaning the car after the journey would support the car's true purpose in preparation for a second journey. Having a dirty car from recent traveling is different from habitually driving around in an unkempt vehicle due to laziness.

Another example might be when a person wears dress not understood by another due to cultural differences and yet both parties are in integrity. For example, a Sikh Indian might wear turban and a non-Sikh, not wear a turban, and yet both are dressed respectfully at the same event.

In different cultures, negotiation and bargaining can present some interesting perspectives of integrity. Integrity can be:

- the strength of reaching trust and agreement on a handshake
- getting things in writing unless you want to be a fool
- agreeing every small detail of a contract
- having a loose agreement and agreeing detail as progress is made
- written contracts which can be relied upon

These examples can be in integrity where people are communicating in a way which is authentic for them. Thus all are true examples of integrity.

In such circumstances, integrity needs to be considered hand in hand with trust. Trust has levels of integrity too. It's in integrity to trust where trust is due. You don't trust someone to be something they are not. If you trust someone to meet your standards and they live by their standards, you are a fool. You need to trust that the other party will be what they can be trusted to be. In some cases, they can be trusted to be untrustworthy. Be realistic.

5.1.9 *Results*

Without integrity nothing works. In leadership, lack of integrity is demonstrated in many ways and it's obvious when you take care to take a look. You know when integrity is present by results. An organization with a high level of integrity will report sustained good financial performance results.

Notice the results ensuing from the way you behave. Notice how other people behave in response to you. How they behave toward you is a result of what you're projecting.

Without integrity, you're like a leaky boat. The results of your behavior are unreliable. Others perceive you as not reliable. You're likely to sink at any moment. You're oft looking like something you're not.

Be honest. There is only so long you can lie or deny the truth. Honesty does count. It's the first step towards getting back to a state of integrity. See the truth and change what needs changing to get back on track.

5.2 Pursuit of Integrity

There's nothing wrong with lack of integrity. It's all around in any given moment. Like any other creatures in nature, human beings are constantly evolving. Improving integrity and maintaining it is a daily lifelong pursuit. It leads to mastery of one's self and mastery of powerful leadership.

It's easy to recognize when leadership is powerful. Things get done. Everything works. Things get done on time. The experience for others, and the products and services produced, are of consistent quality. More opportunities come to powerful leaders because others know they can rely on these leaders to deliver what they say.

With integrity, the law of attraction works powerfully. What you think you're expressing to others is perceived by them because the message is authentic.

Integrity can change for you. How you experience being in integrity at one time in your life can become something else at another time. For example, it's in integrity to wear casual clothes in a casual working occupation. On this occasion, you're showing yourself to be what you are, as someone in an informal role perhaps without leadership responsibility.

In a formal leadership role, casual clothes may not be in integrity if they hide the distinction of leadership. Hiding leadership in an organization can cause confusion with people needing to recognize and relate to leaders.

At other times, clothes have nothing to do with leadership integrity. The distinction of leadership integrity may have more to do with being the strongest voice in a choir, the Master of Ceremonies at an event, the one in front in an underwater diving group. Leadership integrity distinguishes itself by the strength of the following. If the leadership model is authentic, the level of leadership integrity in that situation will cause others to follow.

By contrast, if you pilfer company stores or use company property for your own authorised entertainment, this is not leadership integrity. It's not in integrity for your own sense of integrity to pilfer property. Nor is it in integrity for any leader to ask others to abide by laws that you don't abide by yourself. Maintaining your own leadership integrity is vital to others. When the leadership is out of integrity, this gives others opportunity to follow suit without culpability. It causes security and control measures to be unenforceable. It causes a loss of confidence in the security of a situation generally. Such a situation is not on firm ground and has no reliability.

Sometimes pilfering and fraud may not be the result of leadership example. These behavior breeches can also occur due to leadership denial of the truth and lack of monitoring the resources. If leaders look the other way and pay too much attention to other events, it's an indication that they need to refocus to regain integrity.

Integrity also requires you to disclose conflicts. It's your responsibility to "fess up" and tell others what they don't know, rather than deceiving and manipulating them. There's nothing wrong with having conflicts of interest. It happens sometimes. What's not in integrity is to hide them because you're afraid of what others might think, or you think you can get away with gaining personal rewards from both sides. It never works. You get found out in the end.

Disclose conflicts at the outset when you realize there's a conflict. Give up guilt at what you're hiding and declare your error. Apologize if there's a reason to apologize. This will restore integrity.

For example, telephone charges or petrol charges improperly spent for personal use in a business situation can be acknowledged and non-business charges repaid. Or an extra-marital affair can be acknowledged to restore honor to a relationship even when there is fear that the relationship will never get back on track again. You need to give the injured party a chance to show compassion and possibly distrust you for some time until they see the evidence of your new commitment to consistent integrity.

When you have a chance to restore harmony, acknowledge what happened with sensitivity and apologize without waiting to be "found out". Whenever there's an acknowledgment of what's happened, integrity is regained, maintained, or restored. Integrity is maintaining self-discipline and honesty.

It is very clear to astute people when someone is not in integrity with themselves. If you want to be an effective leader, surround yourself with people who speak straight themselves and who speak straight to you. Be big enough to listen to what others see and you don't.

I am reminded of the Hans Christian Anderson story, *"The Emperor With No Clothes"*. The Emperor was deceived by duplicitous tailors who pretended to him that he was dressed magnificently. Eventually he realized he was naked and couldn't admit it. So he thought it better to continue the procession under the illusion that anyone who couldn't see his clothes was either stupid or incompetent. The fable describes how everyone could see him naked *even if he didn't think they could.*

As a former banker, I recall meeting with colleagues after client meetings and discussing client non-verbal communications to establish the level of integrity in presentations made to us. A lack of integrity can be silently obvious in many ways. People can become uncomfortable physically, for example, when certain subjects are discussed or when certain questions are asked. When you're disclosing information truthfully, you tend to be comfortable discussing the issues no matter how unpalatable the subject. You also take responsibility and volunteer important communication which is clear and unequivocal and delivered in its entirety to the listener.

Integrity commands you to disclose conflicts, declare incomplete information, and misinformation. Without integrity, what you say and who you appear to be are not in synchronicity.

You may fear giving your power away by disclosing the truth to another. However, by full disclosure, you're stepping into your own power with courage and honor. You're showing others respect by giving them a fair choice to respond the way they choose. You're showing stature by being big enough to take whatever the consequences may be. A positive shift in consciousness occurs when you shift into integrity by being completely honest.

Integrity also demands that we take responsibility for the outcomes of our actions, especially when the recipients of those actions have no voice. The law recognizes how extra care must be taken for the welfare of vulnerable children, elders, disabled, and minorities, for example.

Social communities and environmental areas also lack voice. Many times, behavior impact is not visible, or not visible for some time. Or people zone out of the impact of their behavior. Wake up and think about the impact you have beyond what someone else told you to look out for. The world you live in is your world. Take any blinkers off and open up to everything around you. See how you can make a positive difference. Be personally responsible by your own self-motivation.

As Martin Luther King, Jr said, *"The ultimate measure of a man is not where he stands in moments of comfort and convenience but where he stands at times of challenge and controversy."*

5.3 Where the Stakes Are Even Higher

The principles of integrity being lack of pretense, commitment to truth, clarity, and responsibility apply to all areas. If one area is out of integrity, this will be impacting other areas.

5.3.1 Expectations of Registered Professionals

Many professions state principles of integrity for membership. For example, the values of academic integrity are defined as *"commitment, even in the face of adversity, to honesty, trust, fairness, respect, and responsibility."*[24]

---

24 Academic integrity is defined as "a set of values held by the academic community." These values are defined as "commitment, even in the face of adversity, to...honesty, trust, fairness, respect, and responsibility." quote from University of Washington.

Another viewpoint is that integrity is a matter of the expected character of a professional person. The public wants to be able to trust and rely on certain professions and the service they give. It's paramount that all persons who hold themselves out in certain professions act with integrity to maintain profession standards for all members and to maintain public trust.

Integrity requires professional members to be honest. Professionals are required to honor client confidentiality. Professionals need to ensure no conflict of interest in serving clients. This particularly relates to a possible conflict of interest in offering financial opportunities from their knowledge of client confidential information. Professionals have a fiduciary responsibility to protect clients' well-being and must demonstrate independence in financial dealings.

"Integrity can accommodate the inadvertent error and the honest difference of opinion; it cannot accommodate deceit or subordination of principle.

Becoming a CPA, [Certified Public Accountant; or doctor, lawyer, politician, manager] doesn't give someone integrity; rather, integrity is an aspect of character that a person possesses before becoming a CPA, or learns rapidly, because that person desires the advantages of being a CPA."[25]

---

25 Quote from CPA Chartered Public Accountants' Journal (emphasis added).

5.3.2 Public Scrutiny of Integrity

Consider putting yourself through this test: **If it hits the front page of *The Wall Street Journal* and someone you know reads it, are you going to be proud of what you did and said, or what you omitted to say?** Can you stand by your behavior and respect yourself? Such a standard of leadership integrity would be sure to catch a lot of people out.[26]

By ensuring the client receives independent advice, a professional fulfills the obligation to be independent.

Any communications need this high level of integrity. If the communication doesn't stand up to scrutiny, are you sure you want to issue it? There are many examples of internal emails circulated around the Internet to the sender's acute embarrassment after writing something later regretted.

"Integrity and honesty are not optional in a professional role. Acting ethically is mandatory. We have a high degree of responsibility to the public."[27]

5.3.3 Integrity in Management Practices

Integrity must be the key focus for leadership in practice and in management education. Without integrity, ethical frameworks can be misused as manipulative devices to support particular interests.

---

26 There are many examples of internal e-mails circulated around the Internet to the sender's acute embarrassment after writing something later regretted. Howard Schilit, *Financial Shenanigans: How to Detect Accounting Gimmicks and Fraud in Finance.*
27 Howard Schilit (see footnote above*)* reminds us that integrity and honesty are not optional in a professional role such as (CPA).

Taking a narrow rules-orientated approach, focusing on identifying fraudulent reporting or activity, does not give integrity.

Integrity is a corporate responsibility and an individual moral responsibility to take the moral point of view.

5.3.4 *Integrity and Moral Standards*

When I say individual moral responsibility, I don't mean judging others from sanctimonious high ground. I mean the choice, moment to moment, of acting in alignment with your own principles of doing the decent thing, honoring what you said you would do, and taking responsibility beyond what a written contract taken literally would have you do.

If you're in doubt, something is not quite right. A sense of doubt can be so strong, it's almost palpable. A sense of doubt in a critical situation requires deeper thought. Sometimes when you don't know why you feel doubt or don't know what to do about something, it pays to wait until the answer occurs to you. What you slide over can come back to haunt you later. Step more slowly in taking a key decision. Give a key decision the thought it needs. Once a wise decision is made, you can move forward confidently and strongly.

5.3.5 *Continuous Awareness and Action*

Reaching and maintaining standards is a goal which requires ongoing action.

As former Chinese Premier Zhu Rongii said, *"In the modern market economy, operational standards and professional ethics in accounting are extremely important. Honesty and trustworthiness are not only the cornerstone of the market economy. Honesty and trustworthiness is the lifeblood of firms and individuals in the profession."[28]*

Continuous awareness and action apply to all situations where leaders are responsible for outcomes. If leaders want to achieve predictable outcomes with certainty and effectiveness, they need to act like great leaders. Great leaders are conscious of their personal ethics. From an ethical perspective, great leaders make decisions incorporating goals AND have integrity in achieving those goals.

Why achieve a hollow goal to have the result fall apart later?

5.3.6 *Integrity Implies Trust*

As Integrity Bank aptly puts it, "Integrity... Just the mention of the word evokes trust, comfort and a commitment."

Integrity is 100% or nothing. People with integrity evaluate and make decisions with a sense of integrity which influences their actions. As a leader, your integrity affects the integrity of others.

---

28 Reaching and maintaining these standards is a goal, and it's an ongoing course of action.

If you lead with no integrity or very little integrity, you'll attract people who want to operate that way too. People like to be in an environment which matches their own paradigm of a comfort zone.

A person with high integrity working in an organization which is led by people with little integrity eventually has little choice but to become a whistleblower or leave. All people interact within unspoken communication agreements. If someone is out of synchronicity with others, they need to change or find another location.

Integrity implies trust. People trust you to behave the way you represent yourself to be. Trust is not only about doing the right thing with others. Trust is about reliability and predictability. When someone trusts another, they trust the person will behave in an expected way.

A customer can trust a bank which consistently sticks to its promises of service and bank fee levels. Trust becomes a valued experience when reliable service is experienced over time. A banking institution with employees who align themselves with the President's integrity standards and deliver trusted service will have loyal customers who value trust. One follows the other.

People can trust negative outcomes too. In this case, trust can be related to people who can be trusted to act without integrity. An employee not interested in integrity can choose to work for a boss with no integrity and trust that boss to consistently behave with no integrity. Such leaders can be trusted to be:

- acting dishonestly, giving the signal to others that dishonesty is OK
- showing no employee respect, suggesting to managers to act similarly
- overcharging, encouraging employees to dismiss customer satisfaction
- refusing to address critical matters, avoiding impact on others
- not communicating fairly to all employees, sowing the seeds for power factions

- lying to directors or employees to fleece some pockets and rob others
- making false public statements which employees also circulate

5.3.7 Examples

There are many examples in case law of commercial communications or manufacturing product standards lacking integrity. Some are intentional and some are unintentional or mistakes. Either way they have an impact. When the impact is particularly serious, parties will sue for compensation.

Examples of lack of integrity can also be found of academic dishonesty, such as cheating, facilitation, plagiarism and fabrication. Lack of integrity in academia can also have a serious impact when intellectual property is effectively robbed and used by another for pecuniary gain.

Misdemeanors resulting from lack of integrity can apply to any profession, job, or task anywhere.

You've heard the age-old saying that 'a leopard doesn't change his spots'. If you're someone who's known by their actions to have no integrity, others may consider you're incapable of changing from being someone not to be trusted to act decently towards others. You can become known as someone trusted to show no integrity. This matters for your personal life as much as for your business life. People consciously and unconsciously rely on you to be consistently whatever level of integrity you normally show.

If you're ashamed of how you've been, remember leopards are not human beings. You CAN change to be someone trustworthy in the best sense of the word. To be a person of integrity, you need to be that person all over your life. Think of it like a burglar coming into your home. If they come one time and they steal, how do you know whether they'll steal or not the next time? Basically, the reality in life is you need to choose to be one or the other. A person with integrity can be trusted to be fair and honest with others. Or without integrity they can be trusted to be a dishonest person.

In leadership, your own standard of integrity matters. You are most likely to be comfortable leading from your own standards of integrity. Leadership and the practice of integrity is a lifelong conscious choice and practice. Only you can set the standards of integrity and maintain them. It takes awareness, focus, and commitment to maintain your high standards for yourself and throughout an organization. Show how attractive your standards are along with benefits they bring to others and others will effortlessly follow you.

5.3.8 Data Integrity

All businesses are legally required to collect fields of information content about transactions, customers, employees, and business information generally. In some businesses, respect is shown to others, such as employees, suppliers, customers and government departments by the manner of one-to-one communication. Respect is also mirrored in attention to detail while recording data into the information system of an organization. Additional care and respect is given by ensuring privacy of the information database content by preventing unauthorized access.

Conversely, other leaders may speak about providing good service, but don't. In reality, no integrity in data management identifies a leadership lack causing loss of trust in leadership. Loss of trust and ensuant loss of credibility of leadership communications can become a leadership problem. Where there's lack of awareness or lack of understanding of how service is falling short of what others expect, this will be reflected in results.

Against a background of leadership denial or verbal misrepresentation, data content with integrity can identify and highlight:

- poor sales volumes
- low profit margins
- overworked staff taking unusually high sick leave
- high staff turnover
- inability of leadership to maintain viable financial performance
- reduction in credit lines
- falling stock performance
- high cost of borrowing, salary freezes
- redundancies
- falling market share

When results tell you there's a business problem begin to look for lack of integrity. One of the areas to examine is data integrity. It's impossible to successfully manage a business with lack of data integrity.
Signs of lack of data integrity are:

- mistakes in key contact information recorded
- mistakes in transaction records
- multi-user data access outside need to know access controls
- incomplete data recording
- slow data retrieval causing information packets to crash
- lack of information status reporting
- under-investment in information systems
- lack of training and skill development in systems management
- lack of knowledge by senior directors about status of IT system

- lack of backup and recovery systems
- unknown, unreliable, or unworkable backup and recovery systems
- lack of user-friendly reporting medium for required users
- poor integration of customer information databases or fields of data
- poor integration of supplier database information for all required users
- poor integration of employee information databases
- lack of communication between people managing information systems
- high transaction cost of database content
- increasing cost of recording or retrieval database content
- poor monitoring/controls or inefficient database information retrieval
- unfair user fees for essential services controlled by monopoly
- database development in non-standard format to prevent integration
- custom developer source code selection with costly service charges
- lack of database flexibility to adjust to business/organizational future
- database operators working long hours and underachieving service levels
- inability to enforce service level agreements with database contractors
- high level of inadequately handled complaints
- information systems strategy inadequate to meet business needs
- lack of transparent reporting from managers of information database

In business, data integrity assurance is essential.

If each person in an organization took responsibility for what is their responsibility, the collective operations of the organization would be in integrity. How much integrity exists in the organization is strongly influenced by the example set by leadership and by leadership maintaining accountability where it is due.

5.3.9 Do You Have Integrity?

Integrity is assured when:

- what we say happens because we do it or ensure it is done
- what we promise happens the way we say it will
- we commit to a time of delivery with performance guaranteed
- our accounts of what happened are true and fair
- our projections and promises do become reality, and
- where we are wrong, we own up and put it right.

5.3.10 Impact of Lack of Integrity

Without integrity, management decisions live in a leaky boat situation. Without integrity, journey plans are not reliable and making plans has the essence of dreaming. No-one can make long-term plans based on a leaky boat going anywhere. When this happens, uncertainty and risk exists. Leadership is mortally weakened by lack of integrity.

Integrity is also impacted by the way you communicate information. You lack integrity when you avoid conflict rather than be honest. There are many ways to be honest without causing conflict or upset.

5.3.11 Follower Readiness in Leadership

You can fall into the trap of believing others are "not ready" to follow when the real reason followers don't follow is that your leadership is not all it could be. Whenever people don't follow, look at whom you are speaking to, what you are saying, and how you are saying it.

WHO - WHAT – HOW

WHO are people for you?

Are you in the world of the people you are speaking to?

- Is your message presentation style appropriate to your audience?
- Does their response indicate they are willing to hear your message?

WHAT are you saying?

- Can others understand what you say?
- How do you know others understand your message?

HOW are you saying it?

- Is your attitude to others positive?
- Do you yourself believe what you are saying?
- Do others believe you?
- Do you really **want** to make a difference?
- Are you committed to the outcome?
- Have you taken all the steps necessary to have the results you want?

Some age-old suggestions still ring true today for effective communication such as:
Trumpet in a herd of elephants; crow in the company of cocks; bleat in a flock of goats. (Malayan Proverb)

Behind an able man, there are always other able men. (Chinese Proverb)

You cannot be an able leader without able team members upon whom you depend. Your team might include associates, employees, clients, suppliers, or personal friends and family.

5.4 The Test of Integrity

Consider everything we've discussed so far. Review new thoughts and ideas. Think about what areas of your life and your organization you might refresh in the light of what you now think. Create a plan to change the things that need to be changed and accept the things you can't change.

Review this from the perspective of how integrity can be defined:

- Being reliable and trustworthy
- Being someone on whom others can count on to deliver on their word
- Being honest, telling the truth, the whole truth and nothing but the truth – first of all to yourself
- Not doing anything you wouldn't want announced in the media
- Walking your talk. Adhering to the moral principles and standards that you profess. Be what you expect others to be
- Being accountable for your actions
- Taking responsibility for your feelings
- Taking responsibility for the impact on others of what you do or don't do
- Taking responsibility for the silence of nature and your impact on it
- Being responsible for what you say and how you say it

You may read about integrity here and decide you're already a person of integrity. You may think what's said here has nothing much to do with you. If you think deeply about these statements, you'll be able to find a major area of your life out of integrity. Life situations constantly change and paradigms are always capable of changing such that something not previously recognized is suddenly noticed for the first time. Dynamic changes of normal life naturally throw up new areas which need continuous integrity review. Taking responsibility for integrity is a constant and healthy exercise.

If you're already thinking this has nothing to do with you - think again. If you want to be a powerful and effective leader be prepared to look honestly at your life and results of your actions and lack of action. Being willing, or not being willing, to take a good hard look at integrity is in itself a test of leadership.

Take a deep look and you'll see what I mean.

"Be a yardstick of quality. Some people aren't used to an environment where excellence is expected."[29]

5.4.1 Being Reliable and Trustworthy

When someone has integrity, others believe what they say and trust in the stated outcomes. Leadership is natural when others are inspired to follow someone they believe.

Sometimes, you can think you're a reliable and trustworthy person. Take a look at some examples and see if you are:

Some examples of being out of integrity:

- Signing or agreeing a contract and not doing what you agreed
- Saying to wife, husband, partner you'll do tasks you don't do

29 Steve Jobs, CEO Apple Computers (quote from http://thinkexist.com/quotes/steve_jobs/).

- Promising payment by due date and not paying by due date
- Being a licensed driver and breaking the road code
- Promising to cut company costs and not doing it
- Saying you'll prepare a meeting agenda and not doing it well
- Being late
- Looking badly presented
- Being critical of others
- Seeing your children need you and just not bothering
- Seeing your elderly relatives need you and not bothering
- Overriding the needs of your spouse for your own selfishness
- Not bothering to get to know the needs of your spouse
- Not co-operating with another and being self-centered
- Allowing your trash to pollute a river, the air, or land
- Because you can, short changing people who deserve better
- Setting goals and not doing what you said to yourself/others
- Taking on responsibilities and not delivering – for whatever reason

There *will* be areas with lack of integrity in anyone's life and in any organization. If you're willing to look at these questions and acknowledge it also applies to you, you're on the way to being a leader with integrity.

Sometimes when you own up to the truth, it's unpalatable to others and they remonstrate with you. They may be disappointed or angry. Consider their anger and disappointment is their anger and disappointment and it's not yours. How they respond is their choice and their responsibility. You can be disappointed with yourself at letting them down. Allowing reactions of others to put you off being in integrity is not being an inspiring leader.

Sometimes integrity can be admitting that you shouldn't have taken on a task you really couldn't or shouldn't have done. Acknowledge task overload and apologize for disappointing when you've promised beyond your ability to perform. Only you can take a leadership choice in your own life to reduce or diversify your workload to improve integrity and reliability. No-one is going to want to follow a person overwhelmed with work, constantly battling to keep everything on track. This person has no time to focus on leading others forward.

A behavior change in any area which has not been working as well as it could have done will have you feeling more positive. Everyone you meet will be positively impacted by your change of attitude.

6.0 RESPONSIBILITY
IN LEADERSHIP

6.1 Responsibility

We all develop perceptions of what responsibility means, how it applies in our lives, and whether we're keen to take on responsibility or avoid it.

For my own paradigm of responsibility, I used to think of responsibility as a burden to carry on one's shoulders. It was a weight of thoughts when responsibility was expected of me. I would think about everyone else and care for the other members of the team. I thought I was the one accountable for the overall actions of the group. The one who looked after everyone else.

One day I heard someone speak about responsibility and I began to think differently. I am now happy with responsibility. Its concept has a new reality for me. John Kehoe said responsibility is basically the ability to respond.[30] This clarified something for me. I have an ability to respond and I don't have to react to things. I have choices about how I respond. I can think a situation through and choose how to respond. This freed me from reaction to the word "responsibility" but it didn't change the "burden" aspect.

I later realized I don't have to carry anyone else. Other people could pull their weight or take the consequences. It's not my job to carry others. I am doing the other person a disservice to carry them. If I don't step aside and let them work it out for themselves, they'll never have a chance to learn responsibility, will they?

---

30 John Kehoe, *Mindpower.*

Every time I've fallen into my old habit of taking responsibility for someone else instead of confining myself to my own responsibilities, I create I "don't have time" to look after my own responsibilities for me. I need to focus.

Responsibility is now more to do with the question of "what can I be responsible for?" What is it appropriate for me to take responsibility for?

I have the ability to act, react, and respond to events, people, and circumstances. Just because I have this ability, it doesn't mean I need to react in an old pattern of being responsible for others. Instead, I check out what is my responsibility in relation to events, people interactions, and circumstances.

Take a look at some of the following ideas about responsibility and see what relates to your paradigm of responsibility. You might want to make changes as I did. Here are some examples. See what you think about them.

6.2 Reacting to Circumstances

Being responsible is an experience of constant motion. Events keep on changing the experience of responsibility.

IT'S NOT WHAT HAPPENS THAT MATTERS,

IT'S WHAT YOU DO ABOUT IT THAT COUNTS

Here are some proverbs worth considering, which suggest ways of being responsible:

- Don't speak unless you can improve on the silence. (Spanish Proverb)
- The eyes believe themselves; the ears believe other people. (German Proverb)
- A fool finds pleasure in evil conduct, but a man of understanding delights in wisdom. (Miscellaneous Proverb)
- A fool gives full vent to his anger, but a wise man keeps himself under control (Miscellaneous Proverb)
- A fool shows his annoyance at once, but a prudent man overlooks an insult. (Miscellaneous Proverb)
- A half-truth is a whole lie. (Jewish Proverb)
- Hide not your talents, they for use were made. What's a sundial in the shade? (Benjamin Franklin)
- If you must play, decide on three things at the start: the rules of the game, the stakes, and the quitting time. (Chinese proverb)

- If you want to be respected, you must respect yourself. (Spanish Proverb)
- If you would be wealthy, think of saving as well as getting. (Benjamin Franklin)
- Complain to one who can help you. (Yugoslav Proverb)
- Listen, or your tongue will keep you deaf. (Native American Proverb)
- Never give advice unless asked. (German Proverb)
- Never write a letter while you are angry. (Chinese Proverb)
- Use power to curb power. (Chinese Proverb)
- What may be done at any time will be done at no time. (Scottish Proverb)
- What you don't see with your eyes, don't invent with your mouth. (Jewish Proverb)
- You've got to do your own growing, no matter how tall your grandfather was. (Irish Proverb)

Responsibility is clear. One has the ability to respond. One has the choice to react moment to moment. You can react as a knee jerk instinctive response or react with measure, all the while choosing to be happy and aware of possibilities. When one is consciously choosing a response, one is being a leader exercising skill and maturity, inspiring others to follow. The world needs more of this kind of wise response.

For a true leader, motivation comes from inner direction and understanding. A situation becomes an opportunity to be mature and powerful rather than immature or passive in response to people, events, or situations.

Situations occur. We look around. We may think "if not me, who then will lead?" When there is no answer and you see what's to be done, you ARE the one to lead.

Performance improves through self leadership first. When you're leading a group, look out for people who see the possibilities first and act with the leader to create opportunities for others in the group. In this way, you identify emerging leaders. It's also a mark of your leadership when you generate a culture that provides leadership opportunities for everyone in the group to excel. The level of leadership participation of emerging leaders is a mark of your leadership of the group. No person is an island, and without interaction with others you are limited in perceiving new ways of leadership. You'll eventually dry up group creativity, spontaneity and enthusiasm. An organization encouraging emerging leadership openings is a healthy one.

There's also a responsibility on you as a leader to seek ways to draw out the hidden or inexperienced leadership talents of less participating group members. Emerging leadership occurs when the leader has the following characteristics:

- open and inviting of responses
- non-judgmental of others
- avoids personal criticism of anyone
- inclusive of all despite his/her personal preferences or views
- commands respect from others
- encourages brevity and clarity of communication
- causes others to be responsible for their input and actions
- creates forums for discussion
- gives clear direction and invitation access for others to contribute
- trains others to contribute in a meaningful and appropriate way
- shows appreciation of input and results
- provides incentives for others to increase their level of responsibility
- creates group transparency of information gathering and sharing
- waits for others to see the point instead of "giving the answers"
- is a good listener listening for what's said and noticing what's not said
- someone who is open in their body language

- being welcoming of approaches within a discrete style
- being appropriately responsive to others so they feel respected
- is big enough and honest enough to listen to the whistleblower
- someone prepared to take the consequences of his/her own actions
- someone inspiring and motivating of others

Being responsible is being up for something. Watch for results. We are all human. Sometimes you can be surprised by a negative reaction to something you did with good intent.

If others are impacted negatively by something you did, own up and acknowledge it with sensitivity towards them. See the impact on others as you clear the air and let others know you are being responsible toward them. Once milk has been spilt, so to speak, there's no going back on what's done. What's done is done. There's no point in holding onto regret. If the impact is considerable, see if you can find a way to make amends.

Other times an event can cause us to feel emotions and lash out at someone else or blame others for what's happened. Just because you can lash out or criticize, it doesn't mean you have to do it. A good leadership attitude with respect can lead followers toward knowledge of how to behave.

To cause positive results by leading, you need followers. If you want positive followers, be positive. Your natural or consciously developed leadership style can enhance your skills in any role you choose from company director, manager, parent, or social club committee member.

6.3 How to Get Others to Take on Responsibility

Some people you have the privilege to lead naturally take on responsibility without any prompting. How do you get people to *continue* to take such a responsible attitude?

- Show others respect
- Communicate in a way that others can relate to you
- Express worthwhile communication. Don't just fill the space
- In every word you write or utter, know fully *why* you communicate
- Make sure others get the message
- Give others plenty of room to respond appropriately
- Create plenty of silent pauses for people to think about what's said
- Allow conversation spaces. Ask open-ended questions for others to state their viewpoints
- Give others the right not to listen to you
- Be appreciative of others. They don't have to follow you
- Be someone others are inspired to follow and listen to

There are others who are *not* so willing to take on responsibility. Look to what you can be responsible for which might have an impact on their willingness, or ability, to take on responsibility.

- Present yourself in a way to be of interest to others
- Present your communication to be clearly understood
- Be willing to listen to others
- Be straight with others about who you are
- Be careful about what you say and how you say it
- Be willing to understand the viewpoint of others
- Be clear you're willing to lead
- Be someone others are keen to follow
- Be patient
- Give others support/resources to enable others to exercise choice
- Be firm and commanding of leadership
- Be humorous
- Be inclusive of diversity
- Be unwilling to give up commitment to the goals; be determined to succeed
- Let go when it's right to let go; you don't have to always win
- Be flexible and willing to find others who *are* willing to follow
- Be willing to have others reject you and your ideas. You don't have to be right. They can be wrong and still be right in their world. It's not your right to force others to change
- Show your unique talents such that others are keen to follow your personal leadership

At some times, unless you're a dictator, it's important to let go and allow others the free choice *not* to follow you and *not* to choose to take on responsibility. Leadership doesn't work unless responsibility is carried and delegated willingly. If others don't want to take responsibility, the conversation is probably better ended. How it ends may leave the possibility of another chance another time. Or it may mean for example, following a staff performance review, someone has to leave the team. There is no point in trying to force co-operation. Forcing someone where they don't want to go can generate resistance, criticism, and mutual disrespect. If you review and act upon the ways known to you to cause someone else to take up their responsibilities, and they don't take on responsibilities, let go of your attachment to what they do or don't do. It's not your job. It's their job to take up what is theirs to do. If they decline, keep walking forward in your own life or business without them.

Another circumstance is when a relationship is *new* and the parties haven't related with responsibility toward or in proximity to each other before. In a new relationship, there's all of the above to be responsible for in causing others to follow you and take on responsibility, and in addition:

- Establish a relationship such that the other party trusts you
- Decide whether you trust the other party. Be prepared to pay the consequences if you trust people not worthy of your trust
- Ensure your communication is acknowledged
- Don't proceed without being clear that both parties agree
- Don't promise what you can't deliver
- Establish leadership credibility
- Establish project or proposition credibility
- Gain an understanding of the perceptions of others
- Make sure the expectations of both parties are understood and agreed
- Check again by asking the other person what they think you've agreed
- Cause a course of action to be communicated and agreed
- Notice and work with natural group communication and integration

- Discover the unique group problem solving skills and relationships
- Ensure individual leadership is aligned to overall group leadership
- Galvanize group/others' commitment and activity levels

If you are the leader, particularly if it's your idea or business, you are THE ONE to "make it happen". You ARE responsible for causing your ideas to come to fruition. Others are responsible for how WELL it works once you've set the stage and the tone. If you aren't the foremost leader, your role is just as vital to "make it happen" since every person is a leader within any relationship, and each person has a unique role to play in the whole. How well each individual chooses to take on responsibility impacts on the whole.

"If you must play, decide on three things at the start: the rules of the game, the stakes, and the quitting time." Chinese proverb
There will always be "blips" along the way. How you as the leader respond to those blips will determine whether you succeed and whether others in the group work closely and effectively with you.

There's also the impact of perception. Perception of course is derived from the eye of the beholder. As a leader, you're not responsible for what other people choose to perceive of you or your actions. However, if you want to impact as a leader, then it would be lacking responsibility to ignore the possible perceptions of others when you act.

It's your responsibility to consider the impact of your leadership on others. Leadership is not an ego boost role. If one rides an ego boost, it'll be a short ride. Rather, one could consider consulting with others about the likely impact of the proposed action, or test your ideas on a few key people before launching forth on the group. It also pays to listen to peoples' responses; particularly when you detect they're not being fulsome in their reply. This can be a hint that they're not enamored of your proposals.

What you can do is couch your proposals in such a way as to be heard receptively by your target audience. As a leader, you have the opportunity to be a center of influence. You can get to know your audience and speak to their needs at the same time as making your own proposals. Communication can then be win-win, rather than a remote directive, or a personal goal to be imposed on others. Co-operation is easy to get if you know how.

At the same time, there are some circumstances where it's important to go against the common perception of a situation. You may need to take a stand and illuminate an alternative point of view. If you want to be heard in this situation, you also need to consider the impact of perception of others about you. People may not see the world through your eyes. If your credibility with them is high, they are more likely to listen and consider a change.

Sometimes your credibility can be enhanced purely because of your stand for something which needs to be raised, changed, or considered despite the general group perceptions of the status quo. Many will recognize it takes courage, intelligence, and astuteness to identify something not perceived by others, or even perceived by others, but not brought to the attention of the group.

Taking a stand against common perceptions will be listened to at a management level if:

- you first cause others to see the need to hear you
- you use a communication style which suits the culture of the listeners
- you speak without attachment to the answer
- you let go of needing others to change their perceptions for you
- you're honest in believing the truth of your subject matter

Find a way for others to reach where you have reached in understanding the issues, and communicate that path to them.

Use influence versus authority in leadership for greater success.

6.4 Leadership Responsibility Situations

6.4.1 Can You Lead If Others Refuse to Follow?

You can't lead where others refuse to follow. Leadership is in breakdown.

There could be several reasons for this:

- Leadership may need replacement by someone else.
- You could be driving in the wrong direction.
- Your focus doesn't match aspirations of the potential group following.

6.4.2 Credibility Can Make or Break a Leader

A leader only exists in the listening of others. If others don't believe what you say or they don't believe you can do it, they won't follow or buy what you offer. If others don't believe the benefits of the product, direction, or project you're trying to sell them, they won't buy it. If they don't believe you, it's because you have no credibility with this audience. Without credibility, you won't get anyone to take on anything or buy anything. The exception being a person with no credibility can cause followers with an equal lack of credibility. People with commonality will join together.

Where there's lack of credibility, you may get followers for a time. Lack of credibility leaders may bring short term gains. Sooner or later leadership with no credibility becomes a demonstration of unsustainable leadership leading ultimately to failure.

6.4.3 Anger Management

When anger is the reaction to suggestions, you may want to consider why someone is reacting. For example, you may react with anger against responses that don't suit your leadership agenda. If this is the case, look to yourself instead of being angry with others. Anger is an expression of frustration or disappointment when another outcome is expected.

- Were you realistic to expect the outcome which now angers you?
- Were you responsible for a miscommunication which caused it?

- Is anger the habitual way you respond to what you don't like to hear?
- What was your part in causing this situation?
- Do other people need help and support to meet your expectations?
- Is anger unusual? Or is it a pattern that you get angry easily?
- Does this situation or pattern repeat for you and not for others?
- Is the other person dumping their anger on you?
- Or are you dumping your anger with the world onto them?
- What is anger going achieve in this situation?
- Is anger a cover-up for another true emotion? Despair, sadness, powerlessness?
- Can you replace anger with another useful emotion and move on?
- What can you agree upon to avoid repeating such angry situations?

If you exercise no personal restraint in expressing your frustration with others, you may have an anger management problem. If you don't get resolution of your anger from answers to the kind of questions above, consider taking professional help from an anger management counselor.

Where there's lack of anger self-control, one is interacting with a lack of responsibility. This can lead to angry expressions becoming the normal group communication style which is not healthy or productive.

6.4.4 Diversity Affects Management

Where there are variant sub groups within a group, effective leadership is responsible for causing the whole group to relate inclusively and effectively.

Cultural sub groups are part of world culture and naturally occur in any organization. Different cultural groups can be male and female, colored or white, American or non-American, Arab or non-Arab, Asian or non-Asian, Chinese or non-Chinese, Latino or non-Latino, Maori or non-Maori, Buddhist Christian, Muslim or Jew, young or old, able-bodied or disabled, professionally trained and not professionally trained, public school or private school, mono- or multilingual speakers, high paid or low paid, fit or unfit. The group you lead can come from widely diverse social groups. To be successful, you need to respect diversity needs in choosing your behavior styles and content of communications. Show a leadership example which acknowledges and values the diversity backgrounds.

Without a conscious effort to adjust leadership communication style and show leadership example acknowledging different subgroups, leadership potential for success is not maximized. There's a lack of management responsibility where leadership ignores the interests and communication needs of any subgroup. The outcomes of leadership of a diverse group can be limited by ignorance prevailing about the needs of this group. You can be sure this will show up in underperforming or unhappy outcomes.

6.4.5 Listening Skills Affect Ability to Be Responsible

If you're not listening, you won't pick up opportunities for feedback. Without being aware of feedback, you're limited in being able to relate to others. If you want to align anyone to your leadership, you need to create opportunities for people to communicate with you. You need to commit to act on information which adds value to others. No-one will align to leadership where the leader is not listening.

- Listen or your tongue will keep you deaf (Native American Proverb)
- He who knows little quickly tells it (Italian Proverb)

6.4.6 Leadership Carries Ethical Responsibilities

Just because "you can", it doesn't mean you have to. Rather than rob by what's available from a position of privilege, it's inherent in an admirable leader to use discretion and to exercise responsibility about possible outcomes of his/her behavior. Ethical responsibility requires leadership by example in maintaining ethical standards and for leaders to demand the same of others. With ethically clean hands, leaders can effectively handle misdemeanors of others. Situations to be handled might include managing people who take more than their fair share, commit fraud, steal, commit petty crime, lie, have sex at work, have sex with colleagues outside work which compromises their authority, are bullies towards others, or who live in denial.

Organizations are required at law to manage CSR (Corporate Social Responsibility). There is the added incentive to protect business reputation and stock value by active CSR compliance and organizational management.

Effective CSR leadership requires personal responsibility for ethical behavior, setting standards of integrity, and a requirement for systems which ensure an organization meets CSR standards. CSR policies are designed to protect workers rights and to protect the natural environment on which humans and organizations impact. Successful leadership today demands meeting basic CSR requirements. It also requires strategic planning and execution to show active authentic responsibility for the impact on people, a stable performance of stakeholder assets, and protection of the planet.

The planet is a living organism. If leaders today kill the planet, the possibility of continuation of human life is unsustainable. Decadence from human thoughtlessness and lack of education is rapidly destroying natural habitats, not only for wild animals but also for human habitation. Take time to consider your leadership opportunity. Consider what you can do to reverse human degradation of the planet. Restore what will otherwise be lost forever.

Leadership today must be compliant with the legal minimum standards required. As well leadership needs to be outstanding in understanding:

- the needs of people
- the needs of the planet for life to be sustained on earth
- the needs of investors for long-term financially sustainable business

Your leadership needs to meet the user requirements of all these participants in business for you to be successful.

6.4.7 Gender Leadership from Self-Perceived Power

Sometimes leaders inherit positions of power due to sociological historical patterns. Leaders may persuade themselves that they have the right to the leadership power they exert. In truth, no leader has any right over any other person. Leadership is a state of being and can only be successful where it's earned and exercised with respect and responsibility.

Men over women is an example of a group in society who sometimes act as if their gender gives them added rights. Other examples of self-perceived power over another can be: white over colored, outspoken over quiet persons, young over old, healthy over sick, socially connected over less affluent, wealthy over poor, well-educated against less educated, and so on.

Note the terminology 'self-perceived power'. Self-perceived power is an unsustainable model and is only sustained as long as there is societal agreement to such an artificial situation. Once the social agreement changes and there are less followers, leadership based on self-perceived power loses its power and such inauthentic leadership proves how unsustainable it is.

7.0 REINVENTING LEADERSHIP

So you've seen some old paradigms of how leadership can be mentally constructed from limited thinking. You may have realized by reading Reinventing Leadership how you came to conclusions and judgments previously which you don't need anymore. You've had a good look at yourself and become more in touch with your body, your feelings, and the truth of how you appear to yourself and others. And you've made an action list and created a plan to make changes. You also realize that good leadership needs responsibility and integrity. We will now revisit ways of reinventing leadership.

As we said before, successful leadership requires:

SELF-KNOWLEDGE – RESPONSIBILITY – COMMITMENT

Outstanding Leadership requires:

- A leadership context
- Recognition of paradigms
- Results
- Silent listening
- Care for others
- Care of the planet
- Management of anger and criticism
- Reflection
- Constantly reinventing leadership
- Focus and goals
- Conscious choices
- Strategy and planning
- Review and acknowledgment
- Giving appreciation

7.1 Leadership – Recognition of Paradigms

To recap, if you want people to follow your lead relate to them in a way in which they can perceive and respond to your leadership. Relate powerfully and effectively. Start by relating to yourself as a leader. You're the only one who can manage the leadership context of your leadership.

To be confident and sure-footed, take a hard look at yourself and see what can be brought out of you to contribute to others. You decide and you cause your own potential to be seen by others.

Everything in your life is a mirror of your inner thoughts and attitudes. You can change everything by recognizing your thinking and by choosing to think different thoughts.

Have the courage to change what you can, the grace to accept what you can't change, and the wisdom to know the difference between the two.[31] Be happy with yourself as you are and as you aren't. Don't hide the truth from yourself or others.

Look at other areas in your life and business impacted by leadership:

- What are the outcomes you can identify and measure?
- What do these outcomes indicate?

---

31 Serenity Prayer

- How satisfied are you with the outcomes?
- What are the outcome possibilities with leadership improvements?
- What are the most important areas to work on?
- List the areas you want to work on.

You might like to start by identifying what will produce the greatest results for least effort; applying the 80/20 rule.[32]

Once you've created a to-do list and related it to the 80/20 rule, you might revise it again. Try to improve it even more before you start an action plan.

Imagine if you were to work down this whole list what would be the fastest way you could cause results? Said in another way – what things could you do, in what order, to have the most impact in the fastest time, or for the least cost, or both? What 20% could you do to get 80% of the result? List the items in priority for action and cross them off the list as you action your plan.

Sometimes we can be overwhelmed by how much there is to do to make a difference. If this is the case choose one area and start there. Work thoroughly through this area, completing everything there is to do. After that, choose another area. Work methodically through this too. You may not complete everything all the time. By working through areas one at a time, completed tasks will show up and make a difference to your feeling of control, success, satisfaction, and motivation. For example, at home clean up around the front door. Your arrival and exit will begin to feel effortless with nothing in the way.

---

32 The 80/20 rule is a mathematical formulae created in 1906, by Italian economist Vilfredo Pareto, to describe the unequal distribution of wealth in his country. He observed that twenty percent of the people owned eighty percent of the wealth. After Pareto, others observed similar patterns of 80/20 relating to how people used up time and resources for which 80% of the resources produced 20% of the results. And paradoxically, 20% of time and resources produced 80% of the results. The 80/20 rule is always a handy one to use in evaluating results, and when planning how to use time and energy.

For example at work:

- Clear everything off your desk.
- Clean and polish the desk.
- As you put things back again, clean each item before returning it
- Add shine to the cleaning
- Go through your paperwork
- At the very least put papers into stacks to address now and later
- Stack the paper in tidy piles looking geometrically ordered
- Wipe down the phone.
- Enjoy the touch of a fresh desk
- Proceed through the papers needing attention in a methodical manner

Before you know it, your desk will be cleared. Your brain will be cleared too. You'll be able to create something new as you start to manage from a cleared space of leadership.

Feel the satisfaction of being "in control" of one area of your life. Then move to the next and sort that out. One by one, as you tackle tasks and complete them, you'll increasingly change the whole environment you operate in to being orderly and under control. A foundation of such stability will have a significant effect on your ability to tackle more tasks. A clear space allows plenty of creativity without dramas of overlooked things from the past popping up to be dealt with at inopportune times.

At home, go through your wardrobe and give away items you haven't worn for a year. If you don't like wearing clothing articles or don't feel good wearing them, you're going to feel uncomfortable wearing them in the presence of others. An item may remind you of a bad memory. There are many reasons why an article which has worn out its useful life with you can be recycled to others. Leave in your wardrobe only what you need and want. Give away or sell the rest. When you do this exercise, take the opportunity to clean out the wardrobe. Wipe everything down. Repaint or vanish if you feel inclined. Creating a cleared space with a high degree of cleanliness creates room for something good and something new to come into your life. You don't have to fill every space all the time. Leave room for the unplanned and the unexpected.

You could also go around the inventory at work and clear out the old and obsolete. Write down the value and dispose of it. Consider that the space could be taken up with something new of more value on your company books or something more likely to be bought by customers. Why waste good space on something which you've outgrown so to speak?

This clean up also applies to friendships or business associates. At times, it's worth considering the value of each relationship.

Does it serve you to continue with it?
Does it serve the other party?
Sometimes it's important to quietly lose interest and let the friendship go.

Imagine you have a supplier of a particular component for your production line who insists on doing it:

- "their way",
- "the way we've always done it",
- "delivered later than you would like",
- "won't or can't input to your stock management ordering system"
- "doesn't care about a high level of faulty goods"or anything similar which doesn't really work for your company.

When you emerge from being dominated by a supplier who persists in having it their way, you see there are many alternatives which can work better. Try questioning every single aspect of your operation and see what you see.

If you converse with people who gossip, for example, you'll find it hard to attract followers who seek a leader with integrity. When you engage in negativity, positive people don't value what you say. Look at the quality of conversations to observe whether you've outgrown some relationships. You may want to raise your game to a different kind of conversation.

The kind of effective sustainable leadership you seek won't work if you have people in your life who gossip behind your back or backstab others. Counterparts who choose to act out of jealousy or hold out on you emotionally in payback are people you need to recognize and move away from. The same applies to people who sponge off you or your business, financially riding or freeloading on your success. These behaviors cause a drag effect on your ability to progress.

Notice and consider changing your own behaviors which attract unhelpful associates and employees. Like attracts like. There is something you are putting out to others which gives them permission to freeload or be negative around you. Behavior of others can be in response to your own conscious or unconscious self beliefs such as:

- I need to be noticed
- I need to be liked
- I need to be needed
- I'm afraid of being alone
- I'm avoiding criticism and judgment by going along with it
- It's better to pretend than confront the issues
- It's harmless
- I like them thinking I'm kind by my generosity
- It's only the company credit card so I don't care
- It doesn't hurt so it doesn't matter
- I can afford it. They know it and it makes me feel good. Are you sure?

When you look at some relationships and consider whether they're enhancing your life or others' lives, sometimes you decide to have a conversation to clear up a behavior that doesn't work. Other times you quietly let the relationship go. When you let go of what doesn't work for you, it clears a space for more of what does work to come into your life. It's like a wardrobe. There's wardrobe space for people who enhance your life. Fill it with clothes that don't fit and there won't be much room for clothes that do fit. Why waste precious resources with clothes/associates that don't fit?

Have you ever met a person who is:

- "too busy" to listen?
- too busy to fit anything in with you?
- too busy to reply to you?
- whose life is so filled with other people they cannot acknowledge you?
- who can't stop talking about their life to realize other people exist?

When you notice you have a friend or associate like this, ask yourself why you're with them. Possibly they don't care for the interests you have. Or possibly you like to be dominated by someone else's self-centeredness? How important is this busy person to you?

If the busy person is important, then figure out a strategy to break the pattern of being unimportant to them. Choose to give up being invisible. Make sure they notice what you want. Take responsibility for giving them a chance to know what you want, so the relationship can develop to the benefit of both parties. Possibly you need to develop new communication styles, new information content, or new understanding of what interests them. If you realize they're fixed on being busy to the exclusion of you, why are you motivated to be dominated by the self-centeredness of another? Healthy relationships enhance *your* life? You might notice when you look at the state of your relationships that you *are* a person who talks and lives their own life 24/7 to the exclusion of others.

When considering the state of relationships, ask yourself:

- What do I know about him or her?
- What can I remember of what they said to me recently?
- What did I think about that?
- How did I feel about that?
- What did I do about it?
- Did I nod and do nothing?
- How did what they said make me feel?
- Did I listen without hearing, nor remember a word they said to me?
- Do I really know anything about anyone else?
- Do I know what makes them tick? Their likes, dislikes, passions?
- What motivates them to come to work?
- What do they want from me? Is this true? How do I know this is true?
- Whether they're happy or sad?
- Are they satisfied or completely frustrated with ……..?
- What are their personal interests, relationship status, hobbies?

The answer is not what you "think" you know, but what you "really" know from closely listening and being related to others. Ask yourself what is the real evidence on which you based your answers of what you 'think' you know about the other person, or what you think is their opinion.

- Did you assume a meaning from what they said, or did they say that?
- Did they say that, or did you think they said that?
- Did someone else say it and you assumed it was true?
- Did you decide an opinion because of a response?
- Did you ever ask them what they meant?
- When they didn't say, did you decide what they meant?
- Do you now think you're not sure?
- Are you sure they would agree with your opinion of their opinion?

- What evidence do you have for that?

You might note for yourself, or ask them to tell you, is there anything about them or their opinions you've been habitually ignoring or not hearing from them? Other times you might recognize yourself what needs to happen for others to get satisfaction from the communication.

- Are you now going to do something to change unsatisfactory patterns?
- Are you going to check what you're doing is going to be appreciated?
- Can you be relied upon to consider this person and others in future?

To improve a situation or make a change is simply a choice. Choosing is not a mathematical equation, it's a narrative. Choices are made based on who you are, what you believe, and what's important to you. Your choices and the legacy they leave contain the arc of memoir.

If you knew this was the last day of your life, or the last week of your life, would it open up a new horizon of possible changes and outcomes? Of course it would. You'd switch on to living 100% of what's possible RIGHT NOW! You wouldn't wait or procrastinate because you'd miss out. Think of your life like that. Why wait to take action and cause your desired results? It COULD be your last day today. And even if it weren't, how much better is your life when you make the most of it every day?

As the 16th Century adage from John Schot's *Everyman* goes: "time and tide wait for no man".

IS THERE SOMETHING YOU'RE WAITING FOR?

ARE YOU GOING TO ACT NOW BEFORE THE TIDE?

Life today is not a dress rehearsal, it's the real thing. This is it. Time comes around once. This moment and this day will never be repeated. This consciousness can bring a sense of urgency to quicken steps TODAY. Become the extraordinary leader you can be.

- What is your goal?
- How do you plan to get there?
- How are you going to execute the plan?
- How will you know when you've made it?

7.2 Results Speak Louder Than Words

Hopefully you're not still kidding yourself that you're an extraordinary leader without doing the homework to be one. Do the reinventing leadership exercises anyway, whatever you think about them. There IS room for improvement. No matter where you are in the leadership stakes, improved leadership skills will develop from these exercises.

So far, we've been discussing self-knowledge and integrity. Other ways of looking at integrity relate directly to results.

Respectfulness, reliance, and relatedness to others constitute a good place to start a broader conversation about integrity and its relationship to results.

If there's mutual respect between people, communications are going to reach understanding between the parties. Healthy possibility will exist for both parties by each being able to rely on the word of the other. Perhaps you've heard of times past when people could count on the word of a person who "shook (hands) on it"? Mutual respect originates at any time by mutually satisfactory communication patterns. In reaching mutual satisfaction, people take the time to listen closely to each other. In such relationships, it's also natural to respect another in the role of leader or follower.

Can we expect results from leadership based on mutual respect, reliability and effectiveness? When a leader is known for an ability to show others respect, for being reliable, and for being an effective leader, it follows that future outcomes expected by others will occur. If your results are disappointing, look to what's missing in respect, reliability and effectiveness.

How we relate to others is the cornerstone of everything. The context of results is not merely a narrow quantitative calculation; it's a broader understanding of the impact of leadership.

What creates satisfaction also counts. Results are a benchmark of satisfaction levels. If satisfaction is confined to you or a few others in a group activity, group satisfaction is not sustainable. Leadership peters out fairly quickly when 80/20 is to the benefit of a few at the cost of many. Extraordinary leadership creates extraordinary results when satisfaction is "all for one and one for all".[33] Short-lived leadership is not going to be satisfying to you in any case, so why not go about creating a leadership style which continues to develop and flourish? If you have the ability to achieve great things by leadership, why throw away your potential by being greedy or mean? Satisfaction, as an element of leadership, has no integrity when it's not a cornerstone for everyone. One cannot elevate emotions of motivation and excitement towards mutual goals without resolving satisfaction.

Start with yourself. Are you enjoying doing what you do? If you realize you aren't enjoying your work, and never will in this occupation, consider moving to somewhere else more satisfying. If you're dissatisfied, not only will you be unhappy, you'll likely affect others around you with your unhappiness. There's nothing wrong with admitting the need for change of scenery, occupation, or relationship. Others respond more easily and positively to leadership from a personally satisfied person. The authenticity of satisfaction with your role gives you power as a leader.

---

33 Extraordinary leadership creates extraordinary results when satisfaction is "all for one and one for all" as Alexander Dumas so aptly described in the daring escapades of "The Three Musketeers".

Satisfaction in this context does not mean smug, stuck, pampered, spoilt, lazy, indifferent, or unmotivated. Satisfaction means being deeply satisfied and content. It's being a happy person. When you're satisfied, you're more in control of your emotions and responses, and more generous in your listening for others. In this way, by being satisfied, you're more able to listen to others, be related to others, and get the results you want.

Courteous communication by leaders also generates results. Even if you don't get a positive reply to your own courtesy, making the effort to be courteous no matter what, contributes positively to others. Being committed to being courteous leaves an impression with others. Expressing courtesy often leaves an opening for future communications with another.

Listening to the question of another and responding with respect says more about you as a leader than it does about the question. It doesn't matter how trite, stupid, or irrelevant the question may seem to be. Displaying a lack of judgment with courtesy to a question encourages others to see you as an inspiring leader. It's not your job or your right to judge someone else for the questions they ask, or how they ask them. How others ask questions is their choice and their responsibility. Sometimes we rush to judge someone and the truth is we don't understand what they understand and undervalue their communication out of our own ignorance. Successful leadership doesn't judge.

Answering a straight question with a straight answer is the mark of a courageous leader. A leader relied on to give straight and honest communication is more likely to produce greater progress towards goals. Time is not wasted in miscommunication and manipulative game playing. When people know where they stand with you, it's much easier for them to choose to be with you or oppose you. In a group situation, if you can handle questions masterfully, not only does the person asking the question appreciate it, how you answer can allow others greater understanding about the question. A great leader is able to listen to opposition without resisting it. If need be, agree to differ. Skilled leadership handles conversation to allow it to flow to find a natural group consensus, sometimes in an unexpected direction. A leader with a big game plan can facilitate a forum conversation encouraging creativity and fun encouraging others to offer alternative solutions in a transparent sharing communication process. The clarity and openness you generate by your leadership causes a greater possibility of results to be conceived and realized.

Much of the time, people react to their social environment without noticing their reactions. What if you mastered yourself and chose your responses more? What would that be like? Imagine how different the results would be. Such results could be incredibly different from the past.

A spontaneous uncontrolled reaction mode is like reacting to a heater when one moves away to stop being burnt. It's like an automatic reflex action you instinctively do. Or it's like being uncomfortable with a loud music sound. Uncontrolled reaction is like turning the volume down without even thinking when the music is too loud. Or stepping back automatically onto the pavement when a large vehicle is barreling down the road. These are clearly inbuilt reflex mechanisms which work positively to protect you.

By contrast, when you're more aware, you'll notice you don't **need** to instinctively react in many other situations such as:

- with anger "against" slow traffic going more slowly than you want to
- with repulsion or judgment to another person's body or clothes

- with anxiety to a huge assignment two days before the holiday
- with peevishness when speaking up and it didn't seem to count

These reactions are unconscious, stressful negative reactions. All that's between you and stress is you – your thoughts – your reactions – and your level of personal responsibility.

Do you want to be in charge of these? If you do, then notice your feelings when something happens. Notice how others respond to you and how you respond to them. Observe patterns. Choose to be different to the past.

Consider for one moment that you're feeling anger. Change this and instead feel forgiveness, or acceptance, understanding, pragmatism, objectiveness, or any other alternative to anger. Choose in each moment. As you command reactive choice, you'll convey yourself as an extraordinary leader. A leader shifts the conversation to a more powerful platform of considered communication when it's required for the advantage of all.

Unless you actually self-talk yourself and decline the old reaction, you'll react in the same way you always did and the future won't change. Whatever your reactions, they have an impact on others.

BE THE ONE TO BE CONSCIOUS AND EXTRAORDINARY.

CHOOSE IN EACH MOMENT HOW YOU'RE GOING TO REACT.

A kneejerk reaction is an instinctive primal reaction to keep the body safe. This can relate to standing back from a fast train passing for example. There are also knee jerk reactions which result from disturbing incidents in the individual's past. An unresolved unhappy experience can cause anger build up. This anger comes out as a kneejerk reaction to a similar situation today. However, the intensity of the angry reaction may not warrant what's happening today.

Sometimes such an automatic reaction comes out in inappropriate ways. Other times a person's instinctive reaction is an extreme reaction to a minor event. Being highly uncomfortable can build up reactive stress. Get to the bottom of the historical frustration causing stress so it doesn't build up anger and cause problems. You're the only one who can make yourself comfortable with yourself. When you develop yourself to being confident and comfortable in any setting, others will be more comfortable with you.

What do you do to eliminate a gap between desired behavior and current reactive habits?

Someone physically or verbally abusing another may need to raise their awareness of what constitutes abusive behavior. Possibly they're desensitized to pain because they've shut down their own upsetting feelings from being beaten or seeing someone beaten. Therapeutic conversation can change the pattern, allowing the abuser to choose new ways of behavior.

Another reactive person may be fuming with resentment from long standing unfulfilled expectations. A person fuming with resentment may resort to stealing, for example, to meet their unfulfilled needs. Someone wouldn't need to steal if they're satisfied and content. Why would they want more if they had enough? The question to ask is: what constitutes satisfaction here and what can be done to meet the need? Other times, punishment may be required where someone insists on being resentful while refusing to resolve the source of resentment.

Someone being arrogant who can't cope with intimacy may react unfairly against another to avoid showing their own discomfort.

Someone may be consistently arriving late. This could be because they're disorganized or there may be an emotional reason. It may be they're unaware that they have a deficit attention problem. If you observe this person you may notice behaviors which indicate a cry for attention. Find a way to acknowledge this person so they feel valuable. It's up to them to receive appreciation or help. If they refuse to reverse lateness, it's up to them to pay the consequences.

Someone may withdraw from others as a reactive response. Their habitual kneejerk response is to withhold communication about what they think or feel. They would rather live inside their own inner world of fear than take a leap and let others know their thoughts. Fear may come from past emotionally or physically painful events which caused them to fear certain experiences. They may be being intelligently pragmatic. Or they may be avoiding confrontation with someone in this situation who they instinctively feel would not welcome their input. Fear could arise from:

- fear of looking bad
- fear of judgment by others
- fear of looking stupid
- fear of experiencing lack of confidence
- fear of being unloved
- fear of not being included
- fear of physical assault

Sometimes kneejerk behavior can be deeply hidden, such as the person who gossips and appears to have a lot to say, but is unable to speak the truth. This person may be unable to speak truthfully about anything. They may not be able to speak or hear the truth about themselves. They may avoid frank conversation and avoid any possibility of truthful revealing conversation out of panic, fear, lack of confidence, or for financial gain. This kneejerk reaction may result in severe avoidance of responsibility. If you recognize yourself here, decide to change.

The evidence of what you are, and how successful you are is all around you. Results speak louder than words. All you need to do now is be willing to notice and decide you want something better.

7.3 Being with Yourself

By now you'll be getting some insights. You may be angry, you may be relieved, or you may be excited.

Your leadership observations and behavior choices build your self-control and options to think and act in any situation. Listening to your inner voice and inner quiet develops excellent leadership choices and skills.

Being with yourself is an experience which should affect you emotionally. You are amazing. You are an incredible body machine with an amazing mind. You have the ability to create beyond what any of us can predict in this moment. You're at once part of everything that's gone before and everything to come.

When you look at yourself in the mirror and be with your body and your inner self, let all the dross of judgment fall away. Be calm. Experience awareness of your inner strength. Your inner strength will be seen on the outside when you allow it to flourish within and grow strong and clear.

You are resilient, delicate, pulsating with life, able to create in a way where your humanness might be described as "romantic". You're so powerful you can cause emotions which cause your psyche to follow your mind.

Begin to know and feel you are *The One* in your life. The way you are with yourself is the core of leadership. Your life is about you. It becomes a great life when you cause yourself to be related to others in powerful leadership. Your life and your leadership is not just about your personal needs and wants. You get what you truly want by meeting the needs of others as you fulfill what you truly want to be. Your own true unique fullest expression of yourself will naturally fulfill the needs of others when you're right on track with your life purpose.

It's worth looking at all areas of leadership in your life to see how on or off track you are. For example regularly review how you relate to:

- yourself
- your personal relationships
- work relationships
- social relationships
- service relationships
- general public
- media

Being a powerful leader is feeling the presence of you within each and every moment.

Becoming more with yourself can be one of the hardest things in the world. You might habitually go for "distractions" outside of yourself. Distractions can come in ways we don't always recognize. Television watching is not the only distraction to avoid what we ought to be doing for ourselves.

Other distractions can be more subtle than we recognize. For example, you might habitually give your time, attention, or help indiscriminately to others without counting the cost. It may appear the person needs you, or you perceive they need you. And yet your motivation may not truly be about their need at all. It may come from your own neediness to be needed.

Or you might blame your disappointments on others. When in reality, you're blaming others as a way of avoiding being angry with yourself for not fulfilling the potential of your own life. Whatever you're projecting "out there" is a part of you don't yet recognize.

Being powerful is listening to the authentic soul voice of who you really are and what's really right for you. It's being able to loudly hear your inner voice. Be aware and choose how to be in every moment. It's being able to be with whatever's happening without an undesirable habitual kneejerk reaction. When you're aware of yourself within, you're being a Master and you experience your own mastery.

You're master of your life in each moment. What happens in this moment and the next, and the next, is going to be the way you want it to be because you are the master of you.

When you're coming from the power within, doubt, anger, and lack of trust just don't come into existence.

With mastery, there's no spurious behavior or words to fog communication clarity. Energy which used to be wasted on stress is saved for enjoyment. Avarice doesn't occur. Instead there's generosity of attitude and calmness. You know you can have anything you say you want.

Your mind thinks thoughts and (over time) the mental pictures become real as a result of your actions. You see your thoughts broadcast back to you as your life experience plays out. *"You not only create your life with your thoughts [and masterful behavior], but your thoughts add powerfully to the creation of the world. If you thought that you were insignificant and had no power in this world, think again. Your mind is actually shaping the world around you."*[34]

I'm going to guide you through how to have those plans, dreams, expectations, strategies, goals become reality. What you declare in speech and what you think is what happens. *"The game we're winning is the game we're playing."*[35] Here we explain how to recognize the game you're playing and change it if you want to, so that the goals and desires you have actually happen.

34 Dr Fred Alan Wolf in *The Secret* by Rhonda Byrne.
35 Will Steele, Landmark Forum Leader, see www.landmarkeducation.com.

"In alchemy it's stated that whenever we define the space for which we are responsible everything is given us within that space. It's as if the whole Universe comes down and sits at our feet ready to be used for God's Plan on Earth."[36] Once we've reached satisfaction, abundance is enjoyed with excitement, inspiration, motivation, and just plain fun. People behave around us as we would like them to, for our own happiness.

---

36 Reshad Field, *The Invisible Way: A Time to Love-A Time to Die* (ISBN-10: 1852301910; ISBN-13: 978-1852301910).

7.4 The Keys to Successful Leadership

SELF-KNOWLEDGE – RESPONSIBILITY – COMMITMENT

7.5 Personal Mastery & Integrity

Life is a Stage

"All *the world's a stage, and all the men and women merely players.*"[37]
A playwright has an idea, he/she writes a script to invent a performance which tells a story and people are entertained. The ways that people enjoy entertainment vary as widely as the colors of a kaleidoscope. What catches the interest of one will not be so interesting to another.

Look at your life and see that it's a stage and you're the source of the drama. You think of the idea, you write the script, you choose the players to enact the drama, and you command the point of the story. Ask yourself, how do you want people to react in your life?

As I said before, the game you're winning is the game you're playing. When people are not applauding your "performance", then ask yourself the kind of questions William Shakespeare might have asked if no-one laughed at his jokes, no-one clapped at brave performances, and no-one bought a ticket to hear his ideas.

---

37 From *As You Like It*, Act II Scene 7, by playwright William Shakespeare.

When you think about it, no-one made Shakespeare famous and successful, but William Shakespeare himself. First he had some ideas and a dream about what he wanted to communicate and the life he wanted to create for himself. He figured out what people wanted to hear and how they wanted to hear it, so they would listen to what he had to say. As he entertained people, he fulfilled personal needs and desires for his life. It was a kind of symbiotic relationship. His leadership of theater players and promoters was fabulously successful. Everyone involved in the performance had their needs met.

Talking to an audience and speaking meaningless nonsense doesn't cut the mustard. You need to speak what you know, and tell it with sincerity. When you don't know, own up or don't mention it. Before opening your mouth, think about what you're going to say.

- Is this what this audience wants to know?
- Why do they want to know it?
- What difference is it going to make to them to hear your message?
- How do you know they want to know what you're going to say?
- Check the facts on why you think this is what they want to know.
- What do you want them to know by what you say?
- Have you revised your presentation and taken feedback?
- Do others understand what you mean by they way you say it?
- Is what you say important for others to hear?
- Do you know what you're talking about?
- What is the point of your talk? Do you get that across to listeners?
- Does the audience get benefit from hearing you?
- What is your call to action to them?
- Did they respond to call to action?
- By how much did they buy what you said?
- What is the measure of your success?
- Are you memorable to them for valuable reasons?
- Do you debrief your presentations and improve each time?

If you can answer yes to the above, your communication will have integrity. You know what you mean and you mean what you say. It's easy to see when you're off the mark: you'll notice people yawn, think of other things outside the room, jiggle in their seats, avoid eye contact, seem to drift off to sleep, or look really bored, angry, or anxious. Take a look at how your audiences respond to you. Get back into leadership excellence by spotting what needs adjustment. Change what you need to change and be heard and followed.

7.6 Goals

So you don't always achieve what you want the first time? Do you notice successful people move ahead and failures aren't mentioned so much? You don't tend to hear so often how many times people "fail" before they succeed. People don't remember the failures once you've cracked the skills to become successful. Consider for example, Steve Fossett who, in 2002, became the first person to circle the world solo in a balloon (on his *sixth* attempt).[38]

It's easy to set a goal that you know you'll easily achieve. For example, a fit person can easily run a mini-marathon. It's not so easy for an inexperienced restauranteur to manage a successful restaurant, especially when they risk their own funds.

What matters is for you set the goals and create a plan to achieve them. If you win, you win. If you lose, consider it's a learning path to success on the next round. Celebrate the wins and appreciate what you have. When it doesn't work, enjoy the experience of trying, look positively at what you learnt, and reach for a goal again. He who ventures has everything to gain.

---

38 Steve Fossett, self-made business tycoon, who in 2002 became the first person to circle the world solo in a balloon (on his sixth attempt). He set 93 aviation world records ratified by Fédération Aéronautique Internationale, plus 23 sailing world records ratified by the World Sailing Speed Record Council. See http://en.wikipedia.org/wiki/Steve_Fossett.

Try setting some goals now. What is it you want to achieve short and long term? Look at different areas of your life – health, money, relationships, stock performance, leisure, family time, sport, travel, love of nature, education; anything you don't have now which you want. Consider in one column, what you have, and the other column, what you don't have. State

What you want

How? Described in exact detail how you want what you want

- What are the measures which indicate when the goal/s is reached?
- What are the resources you're committing to reach these goals?
- By when will you commit these resources?
- By when you will reach the goals?
- Who can you ask to help you to reach those goals?
- What do you need in extra resources to meet the goals?
- What will it feel like to reach those goals?

In "sowing the seeds" for goals by first mentally creating them and then committing them to writing, you begin a process of creating something you want from nothing. You signal to yourself that you're willing to have that specific goal come into existence. If you don't create goals to start with, nothing will turn up. A clearly described goal along with a committed attitude and action causes goals to become reality. Share your goals and visions with others at work or friends. Create a plan to bring them into reality. Work with the plan and keep referring to it. Gradually the plan will become reality.

If the idea sown doesn't become reality, look at the substance of it to discover what's missing. The idea may be unrealistic. For example if you plan to be a plastic surgeon, don't expect the plan to work if you don't do the training, gain qualifications, and have a positive attitude toward potential clients. Similarly if you want to take on competing with another business player, don't expect it to happen if you don't work out their game and distinguish your game from theirs to make sure you win. If you're lying or pretending to yourself, or lying or pretending to anyone else, your plan is likely to go awry. When you deceive people, you're the one likely to be most deceived. So be honest, and look at the facts. Don't deny or ignore key aspects important for success.

7.7 When Leaders Don't Know Where to Start

Lack of specific experience can handicap leaders beginning the steps towards an end goal. Obstacles can be:
Lack of vision

- Lack of understanding of an emerging situation
- Denial
- Procrastination
- Lack of goals
- Fear of failure
- Fear of criticism
- Inability to communicate effectively
- Inability to align others to the goal
- Meanness
- Perceived lack of resources
- Inability to handle people issues
- Lack of team management

The paralyzing factor which has people "hold back" from being in action is always a FEAR.

7.8 Failure

For many, the biggest fear is a fear of failure. What is failure? Failure is a description that we apply to something which turns out differently from our plan. We have an idea, an expectation, a promise, an outcome which we expected. It didn't happen. So we say that it's "a failure". It was something we wanted and didn't get.

Does this mean we are idiots, useless persons, unreliable performers? Does it mean something was defective or worthless? No. Failure means only that something expected, didn't happen.

Consider that when you're experiencing failure, you're in practice to succeed. You're learning **how** to succeed. You can give up disappointment when you don't at first make it. Not everything works the way we want the first time. As children, we learn this the first time we try to walk and fall down trying. If we give up, get depressed, cry and refuse to try again, we don't walk. If we look ahead and "go for it" again, we learn to walk.

YOU DON'T KNOW EXACTLY HOW TO BE SUCCESSFUL

– UNTIL YOU ARE

THAT IS LIFE

As toddlers, we learn to succeed in walking after picking ourselves off the floor many times. At school, we might have to relearn the lessons of "failure" in a different way. You might have learned the lie at school that "failure" meant being "dumb, useless, worthless, incompetent, or stupid". Sometimes adults in the role of parent or teacher are disappointed by children who don't meet their expectations. The adults, rather than look at the impact of their "adult" behavior towards the children, instead dump their emotional disappointment onto children and label them "failures". In this context, a young person can be left with the feeling that failure means some very negative things. As a result, a young person might create beliefs such as "since I know I am a failure, it's not worth trying again". This belief can underlie all efforts as an adult to succeed. If you're trying, working at it, being diligent, or you have talent and it's not showing up in successful results, an old narrative from your past that you're a failure is still real for you.

To get to the bottom of this, you might be interested to try out a mental exercise from Gerald Jampolsky.[39] Contemplate quietly when you're not having a happy or successful time. Become aware of how you're feeling. Sit quietly and rest, or meditate, and ask yourself "when was the first time in my life I had this feeling?" If you don't get the answer immediately leave it for a day or two. Your subconscious may revive an old memory you haven't recalled since the event. When you've a painful memory, the emotional pain is still there if you buried it. It's quite normal to react to a current event which may not look like your past. Something today which you don't at first recognize may have a similarity to what happened the first time you felt this feeling of failure. You decided the first time you tried this way to be successful, you were a failure. You could never win. Whatever you wanted was never going to happen. When you remember the painful event again, you can see how you've been reacting today to what happened before. When you see the old pattern, you're released from it to live the moment today successfully.

---

39 "How to let go of old, negative belief systems to which we have adapted and how to replace them with positive new ones that work in all areas of our lives": http://www.jerryjampolsky.com/products.html#ChangeYourMind.

Margaret-Jane Howe

One time I was ill at ease with a generous man at work who came to thank me for something I'd done. We knew each other through mutual social friends outside work. He came to my working area to thank me personally for something. I was acutely embarrassed with this "personal" acknowledgment. I was also infuriated with myself for not being able to be "cool". I couldn't understand why I was so embarrassed. I did the Jampolsky exercise.

Out of doing the Jampolsky exercise, a couple of days later I remembered being at school aged six. We pupils lined up two by two to hand in copy books for the teacher to mark. As I put my book down, my best friend put her book beside mine at the teacher's desk. Out of affection, I kissed my friend on the side of her head as I did often to my little sister at home. The teacher was a Roman Catholic nun and her fury was overwhelming. She yelled and screamed at me in front of the class for this kiss. Unknowingly and innocently in that moment, I took on her views of shame and guilt for "kissing in public". As an innocent child, I had no idea what her rage was about. As an adult recalling the memory, I realized that in that moment, at an intuitive level, I had taken on the nun's belief projected onto me with her rage that it was shameful to be "intimate" in public. The teacher's reaction was so frightening that I buried this alive for 27 years! As an adult when I did the Jampolsky exercise, I unearthed this long forgotten memory. Then I could understand my present day embarrassment with a work colleague. I could feel my feelings from the past and get over it. Being close friends and personal with my colleague at work after that was no problem.

188

Sometimes a memory like this can cause you to believe you're a failure. I had another convent teacher who for two years punched me on the top of my head repeatedly with her ringed fist whenever I asked the question 'why?', all the while berating me in class with "Margaret Howe, you are stupid". She had so little respect for me that she couldn't even call me by my proper name. I didn't realize until I was in my 30s, and saw my old school reports, that I'd been either top or second in the class in many subjects at school. Underneath my successes in life, I'd had this undermining feeling I was a failure. When I uncovered this old memory and its impact, I was able to give up someone else's negative belief and be myself. I could take on that I was truly successful and I wasn't anybody else's failure story.

So what does being labeled a failure do to a person? In business, education and politics, failure is very often debilitating. Evolutionary psychologist, Nigel Nicholson, of the London Business School, says: *"It has an incredibly powerful emotional impact [...] It becomes a great burden that prevents you from getting on with your life. You can even start taking responsibility for things which are not your fault."*[40]

Try the Jampolsky exercise and see if it releases you too to step forward and enjoy the success, you richly deserve to experience.

40 See interview given at http://news.bbc.co.uk/1/hi/magazine/4707015.stm.

7.9 How Do Leaders Get Results?

Nothing comes from nothing. Nothing ventured, nothing gained. So you give up procrastination and START!

Start the way you mean to continue. You create an impression about your intentions by the manner in which you proceed. No-one knows at the outset how the future will turn out. If you did, you could go to the future and miss out the present. Everything is in the unknown. If you have reservations about failure, know that whether you failed in the past or not, has nothing to do with the present, except to deliberately learn from the past.

Learn from your mistakes. Study what you could have done better to be more successful each time you step forward in your life. Sports stars, for example, know the key to success is to practice, to study what happened when you didn't win, and change tack to raise the odds of success each time.

People who objectively analyze data, such as statistics, use failure positively. Patterns can be observed and new strategies developed to ensure future results. *"The trick is to separate your identity from your performance,"* says Professor Nicholson.[41]

---

41 See http://news.bbc.co.uk/1/hi/magazine/4707015.stm.

Not everyone can be a success at everything. Evaluating a situation honestly and objectively will soon highlight whether you're pursuing a path likely to be fruitful for you. If the possibility of success is wildly remote, and you can do better pursuing another avenue, what are you getting out of doing it the hard way?

"If it's hard, you're doing it the wrong way" is the advice of one of the most successful yachtswomen, Penny Whiting.[42]

Be rational and objective in evaluating the results. The results tell you everything. If you're getting results, the kind of results you truly want, you're on the right track. If not, try another avenue.

42 See http://www.pennywhiting.co.nz/index.php.

7.10 See Yourself as a Center of Attraction

Seeing yourself as a center of attraction can be a difficult concept to take on if your life runs on an alternative belief. I used to believe that what happened was fate. That accidents happen. Things happen to some people. We have to handle whatever lands on our plate in life. Some people have a lot to handle and some people don't. I've shifted away from these beliefs now. Instead, I recognize I source all of my life as a result of the thoughts I think. I cause what I cause by thoughts I bring into existence.

Understanding how you're a center of attraction enables you to observe yourself much more as an impartial stranger might observe you. In getting to see how we might be responsible for everything that happens in our lives, we can stand back from ourselves. We can look at the movie of our lives without reaction. We can see objectively what's happening to us. We can establish facts more objectively and see what we can take responsibility for.

Create the future YOU want. You are the one to do it!

7.10.1 Being a Big Beaming Device

Imagine an individual as a big satellite dish beaming out waves. Imagine if those waves hit an invisible wall outside and bounced right back again.

Like a satellite beaming its waves out, we can track the first thought that created the outcome we're now dealing with. We can, when we stop to think about it, track back from the event to recall the first thought that sowed the end result.

Tracking back to recall thoughts and statements to the source of today's outcomes gives the opportunity to change lives from being stressed to relaxed. Thoughts are powerful. The germ of a thought grows into a significant outcome. Understanding this and how to be responsible for thoughts provides access to freedom. It's the freedom to change the future.

Understanding and recognizing this connection affords us heightened awareness when we begin to create another unsatisfactory outcome. When you find yourself thinking negative thoughts or thinking in a bad mental direction, rewind the thoughts back to where this started. Start thinking again but differently. Start on another thought train towards the same goal.

For example, if you expect you'll be turned down for bank funding as you go into the bank, guess what the result will be.

If you don't *think* you're thinking you expect to be turned down for funding, and your request for funding is turned down, what do you think? Do you say it's the bank's fault? If you're honest there's a reason on your side why you didn't get the funding. Have you noticed even when funds are short some people and some companies get funding? Why is that? If you don't steer correctly with the rudder of the boat you're sailing, how can you arrive at the port you say is the destination? Your thought leadership and resultant action is the result of your thoughts being the rudder of the boat.

Margaret-Jane Howe

Understanding underlying thought patterns is like taking the reins back into your hands riding masterfully towards the possibility you have in your mind. So make sure what you have in mind is what you want to have. Mastering thought creation and mastering the process of manifestation gives you the ability to perform as an extraordinary leadership.

I'm not saying you have to believe anything I say. I'm asking you to try it. No harm done by trying this out. You might be surprised.

7.10.2 The Experience of Punctuality Is All in the Mind

Imagine I'm anxious about being late. My emotional state will be anxious and everything I do will create anxiety. I'll fit in well with other commuters who decide to feel anxious as we all wait anxiously for the late plane, bus, or gridlock to move on the airport or freeway. Collectively we all create being late and being anxious. What we think powerfully together is what we create. We attract a train company organization which is being late.

Try observing these things. Be conscious of your state of mind as you're going to an appointment. You can choose to shift your mind out of anxiety to being relaxed and happy. Things change when you do.

Try driving round a busy city area to find a car park and being frustrated, angry, and short-tempered. Is it hard to find a car park? You bet. You can choose to switch your mode to being peaceful. Be conscious life is plentiful. Be a clearing for a car park coming your way which suits your needs exactly. Drive slowly. Trust that what you need will show up. Notice things around you more instead of being "reactive" from frustration which has nothing to do with the objective event of parking a car. By being in a calm state of mind, within minutes a car park opportunity shows up easily and effortlessly. Let go of your resistance to receiving and opportunities will flow towards you. I do this kind of mental exercise often. It works!

Getting yourself to a meeting, if you're powerful, clear and confident, you'll have everything prepared, packed, and ready to go at the planned time.
You'll:

- leave early with a healthy margin for traffic error
- know in advance the exact physical location of the appointment
- know car parking locations in proximity to destination
- have phone number for delay notification if needed
- cellphone charged up in case you need to contact people
- be prepared with answers for questions at the meeting
- be "relaxed"

Have you ever noticed when you're being that way, you arrive early and meetings go smoothly? This is exercising the power of the mind. Clearly you are expecting success and you're calm about the outcome.

When you proceed towards a meeting from this successful context, you tend to find if there is a travel delay, the client offers to change time to suit and it suits the client to change time. When you do meet, communications go perfectly. You get the desired result.

We all know how to want to be punctual. Do many of us actively create punctuality? Are we focused and committed to experience an event in the most satisfactory way possible? Just knowing and thinking about punctuality doesn't make us punctual. Being aware and conscious of how we *want* an event to occur, **and** consciously behaving in the way we need to be successful will cause the event to occur punctually.

If we aren't consciously creating an outcome, what will happen? What will happen will be an "old" habit.

The way we behave habitually occurs out of our own creation. It's caused by an unconscious behavior coming from the context or paradigm we're operating from. If one wants a new experience of punctuality, one needs to be prepared to notice the habits and personal experience around punctuality. If punctuality is not occurring change tack and create new habits.

7.10.3 Making Our Choice of Reaction or Response

Try handing in a proposal to your manager and having it returned for more corrections. Or you're a salesperson who tried to make a sale and was turned down. There are several ways you can take this. You can be:

- angry and resentful
- thankful for the feedback
- confused
- not know why the proposal wasn't acceptable
- depressed; you expected rejection anyway

Whatever you think the rejection means, the meaning you give it is often different from what it means to the person who turned it down.

There are many reasons for rejection which don't mean personal failure of the person submitting the proposal or the offer. Often the other party has a situation unknown to you. Some examples are:

- Rejection of an attractive asset offer. The rejected proposal was a set up to leverage the sale price against another favored buyer/seller to influence them to change their bid price.
- A candidate offer never materialized due to undisclosed internal political re-structuring.
- Proposal was never intended to be implemented due to hidden buyer/seller waiting in wings with different agenda. It was engineered to flush out more information.
- Diligent consideration of your new business development proposals was not going to happen whatever you said. Unknown to you, CEO had terminal cancer. Business development not a high priority. He died.

There are a myriad of reasons why a proposal might be rejected. Proposal rejection is not a judgment of you. You don't need to take rejection personally. Good business decisions are based on facts combined with the perceived value to the business.

An important adage to remember is "it's not what happens that counts. It's what you do about it". Things happen. So you presented information or you pitched for business. It didn't hit the mark. It doesn't mean there's anything wrong with what you did. It simply means you didn't get what you wanted.

When you don't get what you want, notice how you respond. Your response can be habitual and may have nothing to do with the real reason behind why you didn't get what you wanted. You may:

- make rejection be about "other people"
- be angry and critical of others who reject your efforts
- be your own harshest critic
- agree with rejection by being self-critical
- get mad and get even by getting what you want a different way
- feel like giving up and drag yourself around for a day or two

- get drunk
- go get laid
- belt out aggression on a tennis court
- do a tough workout

Recognizing a habitual response you or others aren't enjoying is the first step towards getting what you do want. A situation is being created and perhaps it's being created from a habitual pattern of response to event/s by you.

- Do you see what you're contributing to your lack of success?
- Is this the way you often or always react to rejection for example?
- Is this a habitual reaction to a particular person or persons when they don't respond the way you want?

Look at what's just happened and discover what *aspect* of the experience causes you to react like this? Being a great leader, what happened is not as important as what you did about it.

- What did you decide when they did what they did?
- What did you do about it?

You may decide:

- you gave this proposal your all and "they" don't appreciate your efforts
- you're "always" second best to invisible "big boys" lurking
- the company you work for is "useless".
- if you're working for someone else you would've won deal/ promotion
- elsewhere your ideas would be snapped up
- someone has favorites in your company and it's not you
- they're just plain stupid, mean, arrogant, unfair, etc.
- they don't see what you see
- they're old fashioned
- they're blind
- they're not interested

Therefore "it's not my fault".

Failure is never anyone else's fault. To turn failure into success, find an aspect of what happened that you can change for next time. When you see an aspect of failure that you can be responsible for, you've discovered the access to leadership mastery. You know then you can achieve whatever you want.

The outcome of a proposal or suggestion might fail or it might succeed. When something succeeds, this also has its responses and reactions. Sometimes success we've worked for gives us a great burst of enthusiasm and enjoyment. When it's a business success, it may increase remuneration.

Other times success may appear through measurable reports or financial transactions and simultaneously be devoid of the elated feeling of success. Success may give a sense of something missing. It can be frustrating to work so hard and, when you get it, realize this "isn't it".

Sometimes people aren't happy with success because they went about getting it without respect for themselves or others. Sometimes they did something successful and didn't feel the remuneration was worth the effort. Sometimes they've been doing something for someone else to get approval from others. It's not what they would have done had the method or decision making been theirs to take.

What happened, happened. What did we learn from it? What would we consciously repeat or not repeat next time? What would we replace which didn't work? Next time being forearmed is being forewarned. You can be successful and enjoy authentic success.

7.10.4 Examining Your Own Leadership at Each Event

We could consider we're responsible. We're the source of all interactions with others. We can examine our leadership style from this point of view. It doesn't have to be true. We can gain by looking at it this way.

We can look at each event or result and examine it thoroughly. See how we contributed to what happened. We can analytically acknowledge moves which we made contributing to an outcome and how important our leadership style is.
If we can give up reactions and calmly evaluate what happened, we have access to developing extremely effective leadership.

What would quantify extremely effective leadership? One could define it as:
"The impossible is possible when people align with you. When you do things with people, not against them, the amazing resources of the Higher Self within are mobilized."[43]

If we consider that we're all leaders of the sphere we operate in, we're individually responsible for what happens in that sphere. How things happen in that sphere by the effect of each one of us is a leadership paradigm which allows each one of us to be leaders in our lives. We also accept we're being a magnet of attraction. We're creating our part of the group attraction. We choose the responses we make to the group attraction. When we can see how much we are at the cause of, we see how strongly we are cause and effect. We are more aware of what we're doing and how we can change the impact of our thinking for ourselves, others, and the environment.

In today's world where context changes quickly, understanding a situation is crucial to success. Consider a situation from a *context-versus-content* perspective.

---

43 Gita Bellin.

Content leaders are classic head types who feel compelled to draw on their knowledge to add value when meeting with others. Context leaders, on the other hand, add value by recognizing other resources when they enter a room and using them effectively. Operating with a context requires heart and fortitude. Context leaders **need to take the risk of depending on others to add value. They must connect with other people** to have them willing to help them accomplish objectives. It's less important to context leaders to be seen as the cleverest person around. It's more important for them to be able to use their head, heart, and strength of character as the situation requires. A leader can exhibit content leadership on one occasion and context leadership on another.

Apollo 13 demonstrated **what an organization at the top of its form can do.** Effective content *and* context leadership caused Apollo 13 to return to earth from near catastrophe in space. The astronauts and the ground crews came up with one innovation after another. None of these innovations was especially high-tech. What they involved was brilliant use of scarce resources and a magnificent display of teamwork across a large organization. Along with a kind of gutsy decision-making, the true mark of an organization with a high leadership understanding and performance.

By contrast, Enron leadership was poor. Skilling's excuse for his leadership: *"Obviously I'm disappointed. But that's the way the system works."* It was a denial of the truth. Evidence was persuasive for conviction on 19 separate criminal charges.[44]

---

44 Mark Gimein wrote a great analysis of the Enron scandal in Business Week. In *The Skilling Trap*, he hits the nail on the head. He responds to Jeffrey Skilling's comments to reporters on the steps of the courthouse after being convicted of fraud and conspiracy: "Obviously I'm disappointed. But that's the way the system works." Gimein comments: But there's more to it. "That's the way the system works." It's a strange thing for a man to say who has been convicted of 19 separate criminal charges. Reduced to words on a page, you can imagine the tone to be bitter or accusing. But it's not. Nor is it gallows humor, a tip of the hat to the prosecutors who won their case, but something more poignant.

Margaret-Jane Howe

It's easy to blame the system but a system isn't something outside ourselves. "The system" is not some vast unseen force putting pressure on us to do things we don't want to do. **WE ARE THE SYSTEM.** It works that way because we work that way. It won't change until we do. Adding more laws can't protect us from ourselves. The Enron example is a leadership vacuum with no true focus or commitment for organizational success. Instead, there was a lack of character and integrity to maintain the right principles. What made *Enron* possible was not a lack of rules. It was an unwillingness to think about regulation and responsibility in any but the most legalistic terms combined with an unrealistic focus.

Skilling was convicted for basic dishonesty while trying to keep the company's stock afloat so he could personally make more money.

No question, a parade of executives in handcuffs will have some deterrent effect on the behavior of other executives. But evidence that convictions will make executives more accountable and more honest rather than just more careful is thin. Contemporary business culture accepts out-sized compensation as a given, and takes for granted the notion that chief executives have no special responsibilities more pressing than ensuring a fabulously wealthy retirement. In such a culture, it's certain that when the market crests and crash, hundreds of corporate executives at least toy with ways to make numbers look good until they can get their own money out. After *Enron*, will those who go that route may be more cautious in interpreting the law? Can that prevent the next wave of scandals? No. No legalistic reading of securities law is so careful, it avoids the Skilling trap. When you try to keep to the letter of the law while undermining the spirit of law, you're likely to violate the letter in the end.

The Skilling Trap is that trap you fall into when you don't see beyond the letter of the law and use it as a crutch to avoid true leadership responsibility. Sadly, most business laws are in place because we substitute what's legal for what's ethical. They're not the same. It's a tug of war we've all experienced. Ethical addresses what I *should* do. Legal is about what do I *have* to do. In truth, the law addresses ethical and moral responsibilities. However, corporate leadership has many examples of business leaders who use legal advice to justify their unethical decisions. If legal is the only consideration, then *caution* is the watchword. Ethical leadership goes further than the letter of the law encompassing principles and responsibilities.

The issue is failure to deal with the *spirit of the law*. If your actions are right but your attitude is wrong, your actions will eventually catch up with you with a sorry outcome. When leaders are looking out for themselves and only in it for what they can personally get, we will get a parade of *Enrons*. Leadership is about service and looking out for those you are responsible for. Some readers will yawn at the ethical and moral aspects of leadership. A bored attitude will not reduce how imperative attention to this is. The character of leadership is the most significant issue of any organisation. The character of leadership generates consequences critical to failure or success. Which game are you playing? The one for success or the one to eventually end in failure?

NOTICE THE DIFFERENCE IN A PERSON WHO OWNS SELF-RESPECT

8.0 CREATE LEADERSHIP FROM NOTHING

Apollo 13 has been written into the history books as the mission that was the "successful failure". When the Apollo 13 command module failed, the crew was able to use the lunar module as a lifeboat. The management system failed 11 times to correct the Apollo 13 mistakes. Failure was an imminent option after all. The Apollo 13 mission was saved and was labeled a "success" because of the lunar module crew escape system.

Start each project assuming nothing especially about what the outcome to the problem might be. Embark on the process with empathy for the final consumer of the solution. Give as much value to your consideration regardless of whether the end user is an associate, employee, or customer.

10. Life is a Leadership Laboratory

Those you meet everyday will teach you enduring lessons if you just take time to stop, look and listen.

9. Pursue Excellence

No matter what task life hands you, do it well.

8. Don't Pursue Glory; Just Get the Job Done

No job is beneath a Leader.

6. Leaders Need Humility

Humility in a leader is easily seen in a person who knows their own ability while having respect for others, and seeks to lead or guide by example, rather than impose by force.
There is no need for aggression in being an effective leader when one has an inner conviction and the hand of integrity.

7. Life Won't Always Hand You What You Deserve

Sometimes you just have to persevere, even when accolades don't come your way.

5. Anyone Can Be a Hero

Today's rookie could and should be tomorrow's superstar.

4. Take Time to Know Your People

Who are the heroes that walk in your midst?

3. Courtesy Makes a Difference

Be courteous to all around you, regardless of rank or position.

2. Everyone Deserves Respect

All religions and well known sayings about doing unto others as you would have done to you, say basically the same thing.
We do reap what we sow at the end of the day.

1. Be Cautious of Labels

Labels you place on people may define your relationship to them and bound their potential.

©Alicia Yao, M-J Howe

8.1 Leadership Design Thinking Graphic

This graphical presentation gives some ideas about leadership to keep one inspired. Try printing and hanging it as a mind board. The idea is to keep leadership in perspective on a tough day.

8.2 Leader in Action

8.2.1 Act with Intent

Everything we do conveys a message. Know what message you want to convey and orient your entire presence and being around that intent.

8.2.2 Plan

Plan your work, work your plan, and prepare for the inevitable last minute change:

- have a plan
- be prepared
- know your material
- know your team

- anticipate everything may change despite best efforts

Capitalize on, rather than resisting, the opportunity the unexpected presents.

8.2.3 Acknowledge your Own Bias

Up-bringing, private lives, and professional ambitions all influence how we think and lead. Acknowledging our personal biases in leadership builds trust.

Others may not find our biases agreeable, but they'll better understand our intent when we present ourselves authentically.

8.2.4 Distinguish between Process and Task

Whenever your goals exceed your own skills, you need other people. The quickest way to alienate your team is to ignore, or worse, not fully explain your intended process for achieving the goals. With better understanding of the process, you'll have a more committed team. Understand your own skills and limitations. Plan, delegate, create accountability.

Do what you do well and have that be your task. Allow others to do what they do well. Be clear about who does what, when and how. Create flow of communication and flow of task outcomes. Align, re-align, and keep re-aligning from beginning to end of the process.

8.2.5 *Question your Assumptions*

Unquestioned notions about yourself and your team members can undermine your ability to communicate anything to the team.

Don't assume anything. Everyone has a unique paradigm. People's experiences are as different as the number of people being asked.

Everything is dynamic. Keep observing and questioning your assumptions. Your assumptions should continuously go through transformation to be valuable.

8.2.6 *Analyze with Head - Speak with Heart*

To cause movement, action, commitment, a spark of energy or enlightenment, it will require a compelling story that inspires you first. If you offer this to others with passion and optimism, they too will find it infectious.

Success or failure is with you. From the paradigm of responsibility explained, of being responsible for what's attracted to you, what are you attracting?

8.3 Ten Tools for Top Leadership

In reinventing leadership, we consider the following:

In order to remember the ten tools for top leadership, try this anagram...

LOFTY PRINCIPLES

RESTRICT

SALES – CREATIVITY – AND RESULTS - - FOR COSTLY SUMS

Expert leadership is from

SELF-KNOWLEDGE, RESPONSIBILITY, AND COMMITMENT.

8.3.1 Urgency – Life Is Not a Dress Rehearsal

Today will never come again. The past is over and the future begins now. If you want to continue with the past, take no action now. If you desire more, more answers, more satisfaction, more productivity, more fun, more wealth, more advancement of any kind, then take action now. Clues are available on where to begin to have the future you want. Time waits for no person. We are not playing at life and business, this is today, now, and only once.

- Look around you. What's around YOU is a reflection of what's within
- Within is as without
- Create – visualize – plan – goal set – strategize for what you want
- What you have is what you want, even if you don't yet understand it
- The game you're winning is the game you're playing
- Being with yourself can be one of the hardest things in the world
- We go for "distractions" outside of ourselves
- We go for neediness of ourselves or in others
- We go for blaming our disappointment on others
- Where the focus goes, the energy flows
- To be your goal, focus and hunger for who you want to be
- En route have compassion, determination
- Want the thrill of winning

8.3.2 What Is Leadership?

Recap again the context of leadership and recognize where you stand in personal life and business role in leadership. What can you improve on?

- Going forward
- Being the one
- Being the one others turn to
- Listen to others for them to find their own solutions in the conversation
- Seeing the end solution
- Communicating so others are enrolled to take action about your idea
- Gathering support for a good idea, not your own idea
- Having extraordinary courage to go where others fear to tread
- Manifesting resources to enable others to step forward
- Being generous and sharing benefits
- Being a demand to be followed
- Being dictatorial when required
- Being so inspiring that others see and hear you
- Being so inspiring that others see new life possibilities for themselves

What kind of a leader are you being to take care of you and your life?

8.3.3 Reflections of Leadership Are All Around You

If you can't see yourself, look to the responses you get for the truth of who you are as a leader in your business, relationships, parenthood, from your family and friends.

- Notice what you complain about
- What "other people" don't achieve their goals? What can you do about this?
- You or they don't complete tasks
- You or they are rude to customers
- You or they ignore requests
- Do you put things in a big pile of "to do" and don't do them?
- Is something always "in your way" in traffic or office hierarchy?
- Are you always "waiting on" someone else to do something?
- Are "other people" so "feeble" in their presentation style?
- Do you always get left with working late because of "other" people?

At some point in our lives for some, these situations apply more than others. We can consciously be the source of the problems or joy in our lives. The opportunity is always there to be either way. One of the purposes of this book is to recognize, understand, and cause you to improve your leadership ability every day in every way possible. This is a requirement for continuous professional development. The more you understand, the more choices you can exercise. Life becomes much more fulfilling and satisfying the more you see clearly. Seeing clearly enables you to make choices so that what you say, and what happens, are the same.

8.3.4 Access to Perception Awareness

Don't lie to yourself the only person you're fooling is you. If you want a great life, then break out of your previous mindset and realize you need to wake up and get on with what's possible. Richness is not only about money, richness is available to you in every area of your life. Richness is full satisfaction, contentment AND financial riches. You are like the chrysalis of a butterfly. When you begin to truly unfurl, life will never be the same, no matter how old or young you are. New observations and perception grants richness and tapestry, bringing business and personal rewards. Action must follow from increased perception awareness to open up new opportunities.

- Look at the facts, every fact. Be impartial and look closely.
- What you notice is a mirror of yourself
- Remember the example of the ball with multiple segments of colors
- Everyone sees a different picture of the same things
- Keep looking
- Keep looking!
- Look some more!
- Write notes if you need to or want to
- Your day – what you notice - including your dreams

- What you thought of your wife or husband today
- Your children
- Your home
- The day – at daybreak
- Your car
- The newspaper, TV, the radio
- The music you heard
- The sky you saw
- The traffic, the train, the bus this morning
- The in-law
- The out-law
- The lift going up to work
- The desk at work
- The home office desk
- The paper in-tray
- The email in box
- The email outbox
- The deal on the table
- The others in the team
- The boss
- The employee
- The customer
- The supplier
- The spiritual connection with God or Allah today

9.0 CONCLUSION

Leadership is at once a privilege and at the same time a learned skill. It's a privilege to have others trust your judgment to allow you to lead the way in order to cause a group of people to achieve remarkable results. Leadership is also the challenge of how to think and act successfully in changing situations which require different approaches to manage different situations.

Leaders draw on all their life experiences, data, observations, and their ability to interact with others successfully. No one can tell you how to lead. Each person has a unique experience of leadership. How they fare as a leader is obvious by how inspiring their leadership is to others.

Leadership must be grasped as the opportunity presents itself. No great results happen by lack of leadership.

Personal situations have many similarities with business situations.

Business organisations are, after all, groups of people who agree to work in a group for a common business goal, much as social groupings naturally occur. No quantitative business results will occur without great leadership. The success of business leadership is reflected in the immediate financial results AND the sustainability of the long-term business model generated by leadership vision and effective implementation of that vision.

Always look to the results to assess correctly whether leadership is operating to its full potential. If you want satisfaction, respect, stimulation, and acknowledgment, rise to the challenge and be the leader you can become. Work on developing yourself as a leader every day. There are no limits to how far you can go.

LEADERSHIP – THE FINAL WORD FOR NOW

"Leadership comes with responsibility. It is important for you as leaders to harness those responsibilities and ensure that you also empower those around you who scale the mountains with you."[45]

"Extraordinary leadership creates extraordinary results when satisfaction is all for one and one for all."[46]

---

45 Nelson Mandela, 28 August 2007.
46 As Alexander Dumas so aptly described in the daring escapades of "The Three Musketeers".

APPENDIX 1

BAREFACTS   (section 4.1)

NAME   DATE

Purpose of This Exercise

This is to get you grounded and powerful by being connected – starting by being connected to yourself.

By being prepared to look in the mirror and be with yourself, you get re-acquainted with your inner person. If you nurture the inner person and acknowledge yourself, you'll experience being connected, related, and grounded in your life. Being in touch with your inner being is the access to self-acceptance, self-love, satisfaction and contentment. You can then recognize these same positive aspects of others around you. The groundwork for positive and fruitful interaction with others is laid soundly. Leaders can only be leaders when others follow. Followers will follow leaders whom they feel have a sense of personal relatedness to themselves. You need to be connected to yourself to be able to connect and relate to others.

You might start by looking at yourself in a physical mirror. Look deeply.

- Who do you see?

- What does it feel like?

- What is the emotion you see in your eyes?

- What do the clothes communicate about how YOU feel about yourself?

- What is your unhidden body communicating to you?

- How do you feel about posing to yourself?

- Do you know how you posture your body in company?

- Where are hands, arms, shoulders, legs then? where are they now?

- What are you saying in body language?

I'm not talking about the look you give yourself in the mirror as you run out the door, or flash past the company bathroom to check your tie's on straight, hair done, or lipstick on.

I'm talking about taking quiet time by yourself and looking deeply. Looking into the eyes of the person you haven't seen for ages.

What do you realize immediately?

Have you said hello to you anytime over the last 10 or 20 years? Or has that time with yourself for yourself just rushed by? Now is a good time to say hello and get familiar again. You're going on a journey and you need to know who you're talking to, if you want to cause yourself as a great leader.

APPENDIX 2

POSTURE AND BARE APPEARANCE   (section 4.2)

NAME   DATE

WHO DO YOU THINK YOU ARE? Who you think you are is reflected back to you not only in the bathroom mirror but by your success, or lack of it, as a leader. Look at how you and others respond to you. Are you in touch with reality? Or are you living with your body and being oblivious of its feel and appearance because you're stuck in an old paradigm?

Questions -

- Do people's eyes light up when you arrive and they see you and what you're wearing? Can you describe these observations?

- When you're out with others, whom you consider to be superlatively well dressed and presented, do you notice if they are completely at ease with you – or not? If not, why not? Can you describe this?

- Do you find yourself being self-conscious of something about your appearance all the time? Your stomach pokes through your shirt buttons, hair is going bald, neck hairline needs tidying up, glasses are old and old fashioned, shoes need replacing or cleaning, fingernails are bitten or dirty, jowls are bulging over your shirt collar, teeth looking unhealthy, hair in places you don't want it, acne, can't get comfortable with your sore back, or you don't even notice your shoulders all day until you lie down at night and they're screaming with pain from being bunched up all day? Can you describe how it is for you?

- Do you notice the style of your bag, shoes, suit, glasses, wallet are all a mishmash of styles and colors? You feel "cheap"? What does that look and feel like?

- Do you have impeccable clothes but you sweat easily from nervousness? How does that make you feel?

- Do you feel nervous being around others who are not as well presented as you? What does that feel like? How do you behave?

- Are you the one who puts on bravado to cover up what's not obvious to the public? While at home your life is chaos and out of control? What's that like for you?

- Are you the one who puts on social bravado and your bank statements are well colored with red figures? What's that like for you?

- Are you always trying to give the impression you're not

committed to anything or anyone so you don't "miss out" on something else? Do you recognize this pattern now you think about it? Do you know where this behavior originated? What are you getting out of being this way? What are you avoiding? What is the cost to you in developing relationships?

- Do you notice people you admire are completely comfortable being near you physically, or do they keep their distance? What's that like?

- Do you wonder if you've got body odor or bad breath? How do you feel worrying about this? What actions do you take to handle it?

- Do you feel commanding as long as people keep on the other side of the room and nothing remotely personal is said? What's that like for you? What do you think the other people think and feel about you?

- Do you dread going into certain situations like a party, a board meeting, the office, the school gala? How does that make you feel?

- Are there particular clothes you are more - or less - comfortable with? Can you describe that?

- Do you suffer from "can't be bothered!", ridiculing yourself or other people, thinking you're past it? What's that like? What was it like before you began to feel like this?

- Are you listening but not really listening thinking this is all about "other people" it doesn't really apply to me? What is that like? What are you habitual thoughts that have you behave like this?

- Does an old memory of what someone said to you come to mind, something you've not remembered for years? Can you describe that? What emotion do you feel about it?

- Do you want what you see, or despise it? Can you describe this?

- Do you feel sad, happy, curious, or paralyzed with fear? How would you describe this feeling?

- Do you feel excited or confronted to be taking time out for you instead of for everyone else? What does this feel like? How does it change your perspective of future events you can create now that you think about it?

- Anything else?

Take a good long look at your body and see what there is to see there.

POSTURE AND BARE APPEARANCE   (section 4.2)

NAME   **DATE**

- WHO DO I THINK I AM?

- WHO DO I WANT TO BE? (list specific details – create the future you want to see, be, have)

- HOW CAN CAUSE MYSELF TO BE WHO I WANT TO BE?

- WHAT BEHAVIOR WILL I GIVE UP TO GET WHAT I WANT?

- WHAT ACTIONS AM I GOING TO IMPLEMENT TO BRING THIS ABOUT?

- WHAT DO I NEED TO SUPPORT ME TO BE WHAT I WANT TO BE?

- **WHAT EVIDENCE IN MY LIFE WILL CONFIRM FOR ME THAT I HAVE REACHED THE GOALS OF WHO I WANT TO BE?**

- **BY WHAT DATE WILL I REVIEW MY PROGRESS TOWARDS MY GOALS**

Being all that you can be adds power to anything you say or do as a Leader.

APPENDIX 3

WHAT I SEE IN THE MIRROR   (section 4.4)

NAME   DATE

- What I saw of myself at first glance

- What I saw of myself in the clothes I wear to represent myself

- What I didn't see of myself in the clothes I wear to represent myself

- What I saw when I looked into my own eyes and said hello – who is there?

- How long is it since I really looked at myself and said hello?

- What does my hairstyle/haircut/hair color/lack of hair mean to me?

- What does my face and neck represent to me?

- What do my hands represent to me?

- What do my legs represent to me?

- What does any other part of my body which comes to mind represent to me?

- When I am dressed at home – how do I feel in my body?

- When I am dressed socially – how do I feel in my body?

- When I am dressed doing exercise – how do I feel in my body?

- When I am dressed at work – how do I feel in my body?

- When I am dressed or undressed on a beach – how do I feel in my body?

- When I am standing in front of an audience – how do I feel about my body?

- What is the part of my appearance I am comfortable with?

- What is the part of my appearance I am uncomfortable with?

- What do I like/dislike about my physical features?

- What do I like/dislike about my hair?

- What do I like/dislike about my teeth?

- What do I like/dislike about my face, or facial features?

- My shirts?

- My jackets?

- The color of my clothes?

- The cut of my clothes?

- My shoes/stockings?

- My jewelry?

- My trousers/skirt/outfit?

- My tie?

- My casual clothes?

- My dress up evening clothes?

- My work clothes?

- My accessories?

- My travel bag?

- My briefcase?

- My watch?

- My jewelry?

- My hairstyle?

- My makeup?/skin tone?/skin color?/pallor?

- My deodorant/perfume?

- My perfume?/aftershave?

- My belts?

- My coats?

- My hats?

- My scarves?

- My fingernails/rings/gloves/mittens?

- My swimwear?

- My golf/tennis/sports accessories?

- Other?

- Anything else?

ACTIONS I WILL TAKE   BY DATE

EXPECTED RESULTS FROM ACTIONS TAKEN

APPENDIX 4 (1)

BODY HEALTH CHECK (section 5.0)

NAME   **DATE**

Questions

What have you ignored for years, or procrastinated about?

Body	Y/N
Health	Y/N
Physical appearance	Y/N
Emotional state	Y/N
Diet	Y/N
Fluid intake	Y/N
Exercise	Y/N
Environmental stress	Y/N
Relationship stress	Y/N
Medical checkups	Y/N
Eyesight deterioration	Y/N
Hearing deterioration	Y/N
Blood pressure abnormality	Y/N
Cholesterol levels	Y/N
State of toxicity	Y/N
Words of advice from others	Y/N
Development of self-knowledge or health knowledge	Y/N

Write down what you want to focus on - what you've been ignoring/ denying.

1...

2...

3...

4...

5...

6...

7...

8...

9...

10...

11...

12...

13...

14...

15...

16...

17...

18...

19...

20...

What do you see about your state of health? Tell yourself the honest truth. Notice what you never acknowledged before, and what you realize has been staring you in the face for quite a while.

Is it satisfactory to you? Y/N

Could others rely on your state of health for optimum leadership performance? Y/N

What is the impact on you and others of your state of health? What is the impact now?

What is the future likely impact if you keep on ignoring this state of health?

How uncomfortable does your body feel right now on a scale of 1-10?

What have you been getting out of ignoring your state of health up to now?

If you don't attend to health now would it sabotage your goals? Y/N
Can you rely on yourself to achieve your leadership goals in this state of health? Y/N

Do you want to be a successful leader? Y/N

Are you willing to invest in yourself and have a healthy body to achieve your goals? Y/N

What is your plan now to be as healthy as you can possibly be? Be SPECIFIC.

What time, resources and commitment will you commit to your health now?

By when will you commit these resources? (state timetable, dates and times when you will commit time and resources)

How will you recognize your 1st, 2nd, 3rd measurable changes in health?

1..

2..

3..

MAY YOU BE HEALTHY, WEALTHY, AND WISE

APPENDIX 4 (2)

BODY HEALTH CHECK (section 5.0)

Version two – Changing Addictions

NAME   DATE

Write down any health problems that you know of, or are worried about. Write down the daily habitual actions you take which you know jeopardize your health – like smoking, drinking heavily, taking drugs, unprotected sex, sleep deprivation, overeating, not drinking enough water, listening to negative people, or poor diet for example. Write an affirmation about the alternative way you'd rather be. Write this statement somewhere where you can see it often and say it to yourself aloud 10+ times a day, especially when you find yourself on the verge of going back to the old habit.

Example

Habitual unhealthy habit:

Positive statement about this habit:

Smoking   I can enjoy fresh air
                           I love fresh air
                           I love to breathe fully
                           If I feel like a smoke I can drink water
                           I love my body, I breathe deeply and easily
                           I am relaxed, I am peaceful
                           I can run when my lungs are free & relaxed

Sleep deprivation	I am relaxed and letting go
	I am giving up old thinking and letting go
	I breathe deeply and soundly
	I breathe deeply, deeper and deeper
	I am loved and cared for
	I have everything I need

Continue this exercise for yourself on next page. Imagine you're in the situation where your problem arises. Imagine instead you have control of yourself. In your minds eye, feel relaxed, nurtured, satisfied, joyous, no longer needing the source of your addiction. Invent positive statements which inspire and gratify you any time this old habit turns up again – you can be addicted or be free. A position of choice is a position of strength. Invent positive statements which have you feeling satisfied and full without needing the addictive substance or experience. The more times you take the mental choice towards what you DO want, the stronger and more powerful you will be in taking control of yourself. Keep these positive statements handy so you can repeat them to yourself often. Celebrate when you win!

Habitual unhealthy habit:	Positive statements about this habit:
Drinking heavily	....
Drinking toxic liquids	....
Not drinking water daily	....
Eating excessively	....
Eating without enjoyment	....
Eating junk food	....
Eating without good nutrient	....
Eating in pain	....
Gossiping	....
Listening to Gossip	....
Lying	....

Relying on gossip/hearsay ....

Scandal mongering ....

Smoking ....

Sleep Deprivation ....

Spending recklessly ....

Taking drugs ....

Unprotected sex ....

Using other people ....

NAME   DATE

Habitual unhealthy habit: Positive statements
                                 about this habit:

APPENDIX 4 (3)

BODY HEALTH CHECK   (section 5.0)

Version three – Creating Desirable Behaviors

NAME   DATE

Write down actions you don't take which you often think about - like walking, going to the gym, having more rest and recreation, more social time to relax, receiving massage, taking vitamins or any other that you may think of.

Example

Healthy habit I want:	Positive statement about this habit:
Drink more water	When I drink water I am quenched
	I love water. Water makes me feel good
	How fantastic water tastes to me
	I drink water willingly all the time
	I can drink all the water my body needs
Eat fruit and vegetables	I like vegetables
	Fruit is delicious
	Fruit is good looking and tasty

More time with family	My family is important to me
	I am important to my family
	Time with my wife/husband is worth it
	Time with my children is priceless
	Loving my family is everything
	I can enjoy family time when I want to

See yourself involved in these activities. Invent positive statements about them which are realistic and meaningful for you. Create a desire in yourself to enjoy these healthy habits via the statement you invent. Post the statements in key places like your fridge, your diary, your laptop screen, post-it notes. Ask a close friend to remind you on the dates of your intentions. Tell your partner so he/she is inspired to support you in having this become real. Take action to cause it to happen. Create a plan, Diarize it, make bookings, stick to the plan, make it IMPORTANT in your life to enjoy these things.

Healthy habit I want:	Positive statement about this habit:
Acting/singing lessons	....
Act in a local drama club	....
Arrange care family member	....
Buy a yacht and sail it	....
Clean my home garage	....
Clean my car	....
Coach child sports team	....
Donate to charity	....
Drink more water	....
Eat fruit and vegetables	....
Go bird watching	....
Go camping	....
Go on holiday with partner	....
Go the gym each week	....
Have a facial	....
Help out soup kitchen	....

Join bridge club ....

Learn foreign language ....

Learn to sail ....

Play basketball ....

Play the piano ....

Power walk every morning ....

Redesign home garden ....

Renovate home ....

Remember wedding anniversary ....

Train/enter a marathon ....

Take my family skiing ....

Visit favorite city ....

Walk gently every morning ....

Walk the dog ....

CREATE REWARDS FOR NEW HABITS

DECIDE TARGETS FOR WHEN REWARDS ARE DUE

FEEL THE EXCITEMENT OF ENJOYING THE REWARDS

GO FOR IT ! DON'T HOLD BACK !

- Invent a Dream
- Prepare and take action - small beginnings lead to great things
- Enjoy and celebrate small wins
- Learn by your mistakes - prepare and try again
- Expand input resources
- Focus niche areas of development
- Create measurable objectives (MO) - communicate MO to others
- Do what you say
- Overcome obstacles
- Think yourself a winner
- Be a winner

FAMOUS LEADERS

Excerpts from Wikipedia

SIR WINSTON CHURCHILL

Sir Winston Leonard Spencer-**Churchill**, KG, OM, CH, TD, FRS, PC (Can). (1874 – 1965) British politician who served as Prime Minister of the United Kingdom from 1940 -1945 and 1951- 1955. A noted statesman, orator and strategist, and officer in the British Army. A prolific author, he won the *Nobel Prize in Literature* in 1953.

MAHATMA GANDHI

Gandhi (1869 – 1948) nation-changing political and spiritual leader of India and the Indian independence movement. He was the pioneer of Satyagraha—resistance to tyranny through mass civil disobedience, firmly founded upon ahimsa or total non-violence—which led India to independence and inspired movements for civil rights and freedom across the world. Gandhi is commonly known in India and across the world as Mahatma Gandhi (Sanskrit: mahātmā — "Great Soul") and as Bapu (Gujarati: bāpu—"Father").

LEE IACOCCA

Lido Anthony "Lee" **Iacocca** (1924 –) an American industrialist well known for revival of Chrysler car brand in the 1980s when he was the CEO. A well-known businessman in the world during the 1980s. Author and Co-author including "Iacocca: An Autobiography" (with William Novak), and "Where have all the Leaders Gone?"

JOHN F. KENNEDY

John Fitzgerald **Kennedy** (1917 – 1963) thirty-fifth President of the United States, serving from 1961 until his assassination in 1963. Commander of the USS PT-109 during World War II in the South Pacific and Democratic Representative of the State of Massachusetts in the *U.S. House of Representatives* from 1947 to 1953, and U.S. Senate 1953 - 1961. Kennedy defeated former Vice President and Republican candidate Richard Nixon in the 1960 presidential election, one of the closest in American history. To date, he is the only practicing Roman Catholic to be elected President and the only President to have won a Pulitzer Prize. During his Presidency events such as the Bay of Pigs Invasion, the Cuban Missile Crisis, the building of the Berlin Wall, the Space Race, the *American Civil Rights Movement,* and early events of the Vietnam War occurred. There are 21.7m websites mentioning John F. Kennedy listed in the Google search engine. Memory of President John F. Kennedy is strong and his leadership well remembered today.

NELSON MANDELA

Nelson Rolihlahla **Mandela** (1918 –) a former President of South Africa, first to be elected in fully representative democratic elections in 1994. Before his presidency, Mandela was an anti-apartheid activist and leader of the African National Congress and its armed wing Umkhonto we Sizwe. He spent 27 years in prison, much of it in a cell on Robben Island, for spearheading the struggle against apartheid.

Among opponents of apartheid in South Africa and internationally, he became a symbol of freedom and equality, while the apartheid government and nations sympathetic to it condemned him and the ANC as communists and terrorists.

Following his release from prison in 1990, his switch to a policy of reconciliation and negotiation helped lead the transition to multi-racial democracy in South Africa. Since the end of apartheid, he has been widely praised, even by former opponents.

Mandela has received more than one hundred awards over four decades, most notably the Nobel Peace Prize in 1993. He is currently a celebrated elder statesman who continues to voice his opinion on topical issues. In South Africa he is often known as Madiba, an honorary title adopted by elders of Mandela's clan. The title has come to be synonymous with Nelson Mandela.

ANGELA MERKEL

Angela Dorothea **Merkel** (1954 –) is Chancellor of Germany. Merkel leads a Grand coalition with its sister party, the Christian Social Union (CSU), and with the *Social Democratic Party of Germany* (SPD), formed after the 2005 federal election.

Merkel is the first woman to assume the chancellery of reunited Germany and the first woman to lead Germany since it became a modern nation-state in 1871. She is also, as of 2007, the youngest person to be German chancellor since the Second World War. Merkel, considered by *Forbes Magazine* to be the most powerful woman in the world at present, is only the third woman to serve on the G8 after Margaret Thatcher and Kim Campbell, and in 2007 became the second woman to chair a G8 summit after Margaret Thatcher.

In her function as Chancellor of Germany, Merkel was (rotative, 1st term 2007) also president of *The European Council.*

In 2007, Merkel became a Member of the Council of Women World Leaders, a group of women heads of state and government.

ANITA RODDICK

Dame Anita Lucia **Roddick** (1942 – 2007) the founder of *The Body Shop*, a British cosmetics company producing and retailing beauty products that shaped ethical consumerism.

Roddick was involved in activism and campaigning for environmental and social issues. She also founded "Children On The Edge", a charitable organization for disadvantaged children in Eastern Europe and Asia. In 2003, Queen Elizabeth II appointed Roddick a Dame Commander of the Order of the British Empire, and she was officially styled Dame Anita Roddick DBE.

PRESIDENT BARACK OBAMA

Barack Hussein **Obama** (1961 –) 44th President of the United States of America; the first African American to hold this office.

Born to a Kenyan father and an American mother, a graduate of *Columbia University* and *Harvard Law School*, Obama worked as a community organizer, university lecturer, and civil rights lawyer before running for public office. He served in the Illinois Senate from 1997 - 2004, launching his campaign for U.S. Senate in 2003.

He has authored the bestselling books, "Dreams from My Father", "The Audacity of Hope" and... 'Change We Can Believe In'.

CONDOLEEZZA RICE

Condoleezza **Rice** (1954 –) was 66th United States Secretary of State, and the second in the administration of President George W. Bush to hold the office. Rice is the first African American woman, second African American (after Colin Powell, who served before her 2001-2005), and second woman (after Madeleine Albright who served from 1997- 2001) to serve as Secretary of State. Rice was President Bush's National Security Adviser during his first term. Before joining the Bush administration, she was a Professor of political science at *Stanford University* where she served as Provost from 1993 to 1999. During the administration of George H.W. Bush, Rice also served as the Soviet and East European Affairs Adviser during the dissolution of the Soviet Union and German reunification.

GEORGE SOROS

George **Soros** (1930 –) (born Budapest, Hungary as György Schwartz) is an American financial speculator, stock investor, philanthropist, and political activist. He has also promoted democracy in Eastern Europe.

Currently, he is the chairman of *Soros Fund Management* and the *Open Society Institute* and is also a former member of the Board of Directors of the *Council on Foreign Relations.* His support for the Solidarity labor movement in Poland, as well as the Czechoslovakian human rights organization Charter 77, contributed to ending Soviet Union political dominance in those countries. His funding and organization of *Georgia's Rose Revolution* was considered by Russian and Western observers to have been crucial to its success, although Soros said his role has been "greatly exaggerated."

Soros is famously known for "breaking the Bank of England" on Black Wednesday in 1992. With an estimated current net worth of around $8.5 billion, he is ranked by *Forbes* as the 80th-richest person in the world.

He is a well-known philanthropist and published author, including "The Age of Fallibility: Consequences of the War on Terror", "George Soros on Globalization", "Open Society: Reforming Global Capitalism", "The Crisis of Global Capitalism: Open Society Endangered", "Soros on Soros: Staying Ahead of the Curve" and "The Alchemy of Finance".

HUGO CHAVEZ

Hugo Rafael **Chávez** Frías (1954 –) President of Venezuela. As the leader of the Bolivarian Revolution, Chávez promotes his vision of democratic socialism, Latin American integration, and anti-imperialism. He is also a critic of neoliberal globalization and United States foreign policy.

Chávez was elected President in 1998 with a campaign centering on promises of aiding Venezuela's poor majority. Domestically, Chávez has launched Bolivarian Missions, whose goals are to combat disease, illiteracy, malnutrition, poverty, and other social ills. Abroad, Chávez has acted against the Washington Consensus by supporting alternative models of economic development, and has advocated cooperation among the world's poor nations, especially those in Latin America.

Chávez's reforms have evoked controversy in Venezuela and abroad, receiving both vehement criticism and enthusiastic support. Some foreign governments, especially the government of the United States, view Chávez as a threat to democracy in Latin America. Others sympathize with his ideology or welcome his bilateral trade and reciprocal aid agreements. In 2005 and 2006 he was named one of Time magazine's 100 most influential people.

MARJORIE SCARDINO

Dame Marjorie Morris **Scardino**, DBE, FRSA, (1947 –) CEO of *Pearson PLC*. She became the first female Chief Executive of a FTSE 100 company when she was appointed CEO of Pearson in 1997. She is also a non-executive director of *Nokia* and former CEO of *The Economist Group*.

Scardino is a graduate of *Baylor University* and the *University of San Francisco School of Law* and the winner of the 2002 *Benjamin Franklin Medal*. Before 1985 she was the editor of the Pulitzer Prize-winning newspaper, *The Georgia Gazette*.

MIKHAIL GORBACHEV

Mikhail Sergeyevich **Gorbachev** (1931 –) is a Russian politician. He was the last General Secretary of the Communist Party of the Soviet Union, as well as head of state of the USSR, serving from 1985 until its collapse in 1991. His attempts at reform, perestroika and glasnost, as well as summit conferences with United States President Ronald Reagan, contributed to the end of the Cold War, and also ended political supremacy of the Communist Party of the Soviet Union (CPSU) and led to the dissolution of the Soviet Union. He was awarded the Nobel Peace Prize in 1990, and is currently the leader of the Union of Social-Democrats, a political party founded after the official dissolution of the Social Democratic Party of Russia in 2007.

OPRAH WINFREY

Oprah Gail **Winfrey** (1954 –) is the American multiple-Emmy Award winning host of *The Oprah Winfrey Show,* the highest-rated talk show in television history. She is also an influential book critic, an Academy Award-nominated actress, and a magazine publisher. She has been ranked the richest African American of the 20th century, the most philanthropic African American of all time, and the world's only black billionaire for three straight years. She is also, according to some assessments, the most influential woman in the world.

About the Author

Businesswoman Margaret-Jane Howe in business leadership positions throughout her career, collaborates with global business leaders, and observes organizational development and performance. She worked to realize business goals and build functioning teams. Margaret-Jane believes competent and self-aware leaders are the vital ingredient to success. Good leadership,or lack of it, is the margin between under-performing businesses and potential talent development of all team participants. Leadership styles and competence cause full expression and effectiveness of others vital to realization of team goals.

The old adage 'the buck stops here' does not change. The first step to becoming a good leader and to develop leadership in others, is to shape up your own jaded performance or lack of awareness, and look at your own leadership. Reinventing leadership is an opportunity to look what you understand about leadership, how you are living leadership, possibly expand your paradigm of leadership, take a fresh look at what personal potential is underutilized, and see ways to influence others effectively.

Reinventing leadership is not about telling you how to suck eggs. Reinventing leadership is a manual for regular referral to ask yourself questions to reinvent your own leadership and realize your potential as a person. When you are being the best leader you can be you can be sure others will show up around you in strong leadership development. Everyone is capable of leadership if they know how and are given the opportunity.

What would it be like to realize your team's performance beyond what you can imagine is possible in this moment? What would be the impact on you and your personal life to be able to cause others to be accountable, reliable, and sure to perform? How would the business results look? You CAN do it! If you are not on the top of the wave in your business at this time - or not feeling full of vitality - or others are complaining around you - read the book - and get thinking about what you can tune up. Take action on your own life and the world around you will change for the better.

Margaret-Jane Howe provides services to business leaders globally to improve outcomes of business leaders in Asia, Europe, United States, United Kingdom. Margaret-Jane was born in New Zealand, qualified there as Chartered Accountant, graduated from Auckland University, qualified in London IT Engineer with Microsoft, qualified as Master Business and Executive Leadership Coach (affiliated International Coaching Federation). She provides CEO and Director level services one-to-one, business seminars, and business team training.